HANDCUFFED

By Victor S
Copyright © 2015

All rights reserved. No part of this publication may be reproduced, or transmitted, in any form, or by any means (electronic, mechanical, photocopying, recording, or otherwise), without the prior written permission of the copyright owner and the above publisher of this book. Except in the case of any brief quotations embodied in critical reviews and certain other noncommercial uses permitted by copyright laws.

I hope to provide some useful advice to those of you who are thinking about exploring the field of Corrections and for those that are already in the system

You will find that most, if not these things happen daily in a correctional institutional setting.

2 out of 10 correctional officers will experience a stressful situation in their regular workday. 1 out of 10 might be compromised into doing something for an inmate that could cost them their entire career in corrections.

You don't want to fall into this or any kind of trap. We can stop this if we all work together, and try not to compete against your fellow officer.

To my knowledge, law enforcement institutions spend a great amount of time, money and resources to find the right recruits for the job. Pretty soon certain correctional institutions are going to have their recruits go straight to the academy, instead of going through Institutional Familiarization which is done before the academy training.

The real on the job training will soon begin. In some cases, if you leave employment before your probation is over; you might have to pay back thousands of dollars for the academy training you received.

Classes offered:

Self-defense techniques

Policy and procedures

Inmate behavior management

Ethics and professionalism

Offender disciplinary procedures

Listening techniques

Physical fitness

And much more

Staff members must pass a Reading Comprehension test and a Physical Agility test to go to the next process. This consists of push-ups, running, sit-ups and additional exercises.

Nowadays, you start working in a correctional facility before you even start the academy. That is done so you can get familiarized on a hands-on basis with the facility, and its policy and procedures for that institution.

On a professional level, and with precaution, you must learn how to multi-task and deal with different personalities in this kind of environment.

As well as your daily life, outside of the work place when you just may see someone who was an inmate at one time or another.
Break relieving

Have you ever walked into a grocery store or supermarket and come across a cashier who had the worst case of, I don't feel like working here today attitude?

I did.

I was getting ready to pay for my groceries. When I finished swiping my credit card through the credit terminal, she told me in a rude manner, that it was declined. She looked at me like she was pissed off. I said OK, I'll try another card. Swiped my other card and, it worked.

When she gave me the receipt, she handed it to me without looking at my direction.

They usually say thank you, come again. I replied with thank you (with a smile) and said have a nice day while exiting the store.

Who won this battle? I didn't have to say much, as I left the store satisfied with my positive attitude.

I think someone needed an anger management class. She must have been in a bad mood, had some problems at home before she started work and decided to take it out on the customers that day.

Ladies, and gentlemen, employees of all ages, that's not good for business.

Remember, you represent your employer, and you're serving the costumers.

The most enjoyable aspect of being a correctional officer is working with a great staff. People you can communicate with and people who share the same experience as you. You can find great people everywhere.

Visitation: During visiting hours, officers must be on their toes and observe everything. For some, this assignment can be very stressful. There are visitors that might have some hidden contraband that may have gone through security undetected.

Always be aware of any physical contact with any visitors and inmates. If a visitor asked to use the restroom, make sure you and your fellow officers are on the alert. You'd be surprised what you can find in the restroom.

Most of the illegal stuff is brought in from the outside. As with any institution, we are always looking to improve security in all aspects. Not to the fault of any staff members. Some inmates are always looking for a way in or out.

Unfortunately, there are the few times that contraband can get into an institution by fellow officers or other staff members that may have been compromised by an inmate.

If you choose this job for your career or are already an officer, remember to always put your poker face on. Always go home the same way you went to work. In one piece!

The Correctional setting is not for everyone. I once knew a Correctional officer from New York City. He went through the academy, did three years, and then out of nowhere, he quit.

During his employment, he had stated to me that the staff members were great to work with, and the pay and the benefits were not bad at all.

He said he recognized a few too many inmates. While he was at work, some of them even called him by his first name. This is the reason why he left. I understood why. However, under those circumstances, if it were me, I would not quit. In this line of work it's bound to happen.

Just like that annoying relative or friend you don't want to see in your daily life, simply leave it at the door before you start your shift. It was a good thing he was able to get his old job back.

Your personal appearance on the job is very important: Remember how you wore your nice suit to that job interview? You wanted to make a good impression, right?

Wear your uniform the way it's supposed to be worn. No saggy pants.

If you were my boss, would you have liked me to wear my uniform like I slept in it?

Your equipment belt should fit snug but not too tight. For the men, a nicely groomed appearance will suffice. Women, in my opinion, should not wear earrings to work in a correctional setting. This can be a safety issue as one earring could fall off, and sometimes the officer will not even notice. An inmate can pick it up and use it as a weapon. The employer can discipline the individual for not safeguarding personal property.

Would you leave your personal property in a gym locker that is not locked?

Do you know anyone who was always looking for their eye glasses? Then they find out it was right above their eyes, resting on their forehead.

I knew officers that liked to walk around with their car keys dangling on a key chain near their waistband. If you were to lose your car keys, and ended up in an inmate's hand, wouldn't you feel embarrassed?

Treat them (inmates) with respect. Always keep in mind they are after all someone's father, mother, sister, brother Etc.

It's a small world. I once had an inmate-dorm-worker that was a cousin of one of the officers I was working with.

It could very well be one of your own family members. Stay positive, motivated, and alert always. Go home the same way you went to work. "In one piece" with peace of mind.

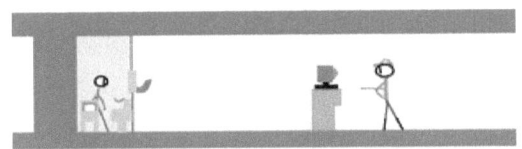

Studies have shown that the life expectancy of a Correction Officer is somewhere around 58 years old due to working in an extremely demanding and stressful environment. The national average, I believe is 75

One contributor to the stress at work can be problems with your fellow coworkers. Another is the inmate population. Take control of your stress level.

If you have a tough skin and you follow all the guidelines provided by your employer at your job site, your days and work nights will go a lot smoother and faster.

Some facilities should come up with a program that can help correctional staff on how to cope with stressful situations. And maybe involve a family member so they can be there for moral support.

A stressful situation can be where an officer has been compromised by an inmate, in doing something he was not supposed to do. You have these programs for the inmates. What about your staff members?

Handcuffing Techniques

Correctional officers are responsible for the safety and security of the inmates and themselves. When transporting an inmate to a hospital, other facility or across the hall to another unit you should handcuff the inmate behind his or her back with palms together or back-to-back. It's much safer for you.

Remember the basic procedures when applying the handcuffs. "Double lock."

Do not carry anything else other than your handcuffs when handcuffing an inmate. If you're carrying a flash light or another item in your hand, like a pen, paper, or other items that can distract you. It can be used as a weapon against you or another inmate if the inmate gets hold of it.

Prepare for the unexpected.

When securing an inmate, always pay attention to your surroundings. As for my own policies at my job for handcuffing, it consists of in the back and double locking when applicable.

Short cuts can be deadly. At the end of the day we all want to go home safe and sound.

Always adhere to the institution's policy. At that moment, we don't say anything because you should wait until you pull your fellow officer quietly to the side and tell him what you observe he is doing wrong. He might thank you later for it.

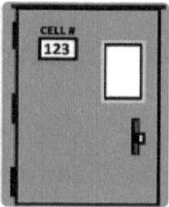

Never take a bad position. When escorting prisoners, stand or walk behind them. Not in front of them. When this happens, inmates can pass contraband to each other.

I have observed this mistake a few too many times when officers were transporting inmates. Escorting from unit to unit and transporting from one facility to another.

I hear this one all the time. CO these cuffs are on too tight. OK! Officers, if they are on too tight make sure you use the pinky finger rule. You have made physical contact with the inmate.

Now, he knows where you are without looking at you. They spend most of their time observing in jail. Double check your handcuffs and double lock.

When working at a jail or prison facility

Use your personal observation. See what you can pick up. Who's the cleanest inmate in your unit?

Which inmate has a history of manipulating staff? Make a list of his actions for future reference. Share your ideas with staff members.

Which inmate greets you upon your arrival to the unit? Which inmate is the loudest of them all?

Which inmate signals the others, to let them know you are approaching their area? Which inmate likes to work out a lot?

Which inmate tells you what he needs, instead of asking? Let me get some paper! Instead of, "Can I get some toilet paper CO?"

Are the inmates giving you a hint as to what's going on in your assigned area? Is there one inmate who usually gives you clues occasionally to incidents that occurred in your unit?

Is the unit too quiet today? Are you going to have the ability to lead, supervise, and instruct the inmates? Remember, you must make decisions and act quickly.

Can you pick out the inmate that wants to tell you something but can't because he's afraid the others might think he's a snitch? When this happens, take him to the side. When all is quiet, ask if everything is OK. I'm not a mind reader. But I can, at times, read body language.

Which inmate likes to fake being ill just to see the nurse? Which inmate criticizes the way you handle certain situations in the unit, then talks to your supervisors about it?

Pay close attention to the inmate that has been in his cell or bed assignment all day since you started your shift. Did you bother to find out if he's ok? What have you learned from him? Does he take medication?

Striking up a good conversation with an inmate can be helpful:

The inmates usually will know what kind of day they will have depending on what officer takes over their pod or unit.

Be assertive in your verbal communication.

Take your time to learn about the job you are about to do. In the long run, it can save your life.

Don't ignore warning signs:

Be alert. Be aware of your surroundings. At any given moment, anything can happen.

Two inmates were having an argument on a top tier. I knew it was going to escalate because of the way they were approaching each other. At the same time, while I was at my desk, I had another inmate ask me for toilet paper. He knew what was about to happen to the other two. It was a ploy to distract me. It didn't work. The situation was handled in a professional manner.

Always proceed with caution. A room full of quiet inmates can, at times, be a warning sign that something happened or is going to happen.

It can also mean, that the officer you are about to relieve has them quiet until you get there. When this happens, look for inmates that are in their assigned bunks and do not show their face, because they might have a mark on their facial area. You rather be safe than sorry.

Usually, these inmates will make believe they are sleeping during your whole shift.

Don't go to work tired or preoccupied with non- work-related thoughts:

Leave your family business at home. At times, the inmates can tell if you are happy, energetic or angry. Has anything changed in your daily routine?

When reporting for duty always put your work game face on. At the local, State and Federal level, we all supervise inmate activities and maintain good order.

When Searching prisoners or detainees and their cells: Be firm, fair and consistent always. A prison environment can be a bit overwhelming at times. Keep your cool. You can ask the inmate if he has anything that is unauthorized on his person that can cause harm to you or to him.

Inmate Distractions:

1) An inmate is talking to himself out loud.
2) An inmate is walking in the pod wearing his uniform improperly.
3) Sitting or standing on the tables.
4) Being disorderly during headcount.
5) Wearing unauthorized items on the head. Shirt, a pair of socks used as a bandana, and rubber bands on their wrist.
6) An inmate walks up to you to ask you a question that you can't answer. A ploy to get personal information on you.
7) Two inmates go to opposite sides of your desk, to ask for the same thing every five minutes.
8) Inmates asking you for the time, when they know there is a clock on the wall.
9) Using profane language (In a loud voice) while on the phone.
10) Yelling across the unit trying to show off in front of other inmates.
11) Inmates pushing each other in a playful manner. They appear to be fighting each other. Therefore, we have rules: No horseplay.

12) Inmates throwing objects across the unit.
13) Display of extreme rage.
14) Damaging of jail property: chairs, tables, phones or unusual behavior, is another sign an inmate wants to leave the unit or as they say, "Checking off."
15) A couple of inmates are talking to each other in a disruptive manner.
16) Inmates are sitting on the staircase instead of a chair.

Becoming knowledgeable with the inmates and their behavior:

Observe and recall inmate behavior, their surroundings and events.

Do you know of any inmates who talk to themselves?

Can you tell which inmate is a pod boss? Which inmate runs a store from his cell or locker?

Which one likes to gamble?

Which inmate stays awake all night reading a book, while the other inmates are sleeping?

All inmates are not alike. Take time to understand them. It might sound foolish, but you can also learn from them.

I have learned how to use canteen items as a weapon. Kitchen utensil as a razor for shaving.

Interact with inmates to establish and maintain an effective working environment.

Ability to think and act quickly during any emergency is a must. What's the first thing that comes to your mind, when you see two inmates fighting?

Capacity to remain calm during any situation is to your benefit for everyone's safety.

Keeping inmates occupied with productive activities, can show you what they can do. Some facilities have a High School program where inmates can obtain their diploma.

Even though you're not interested, carefully listen to what others must say. The inmates will hold you accountable for what you say.
Some inmates like to talk about the positive things they did before they were incarcerated.
This could be a sign the he wants to do good for himself.

You could find yourself in one of these scenarios. So always proceed with caution.

S1: You are about to start your night shift. You arrive at your assigned post at approximately 11pm. Suddenly you see the officer you are about to relieve sitting behind the desk looking at the computer. You know it's time for her to go home.

You also notice that a trustee, (inmate worker/dorm janitor) is cleaning a locker that's right behind her.

Usually, depending on what facility you are working for, all officers are supposed to have the inmates in their assigned cells before you take over the assigned post. The officer you are about to relieve acts like she's surprised to see you. The trustee is looking at you with a surprised facial expression and greets you with, "Hey what up CO?" Priceless!

Maybe, he was just cleaning the office. The other inmates in the unit are locked in their cell for the night. Leave no witnesses, huh? You tell the inmate to go back to his cell, and wait till you call him out.

As per the post orders, no inmates are to be out after lockdown. The Inmate then complies. He quietly goes to his cell without hesitation. The officer hands you her logbook and the dorm keys. She quietly leaves the dorm and says, see you next time.

My vacation starts today she stated in a normal tone, but some inmates heard what she said because some of the cells are right next to the office. Personally, I would have been ready to leave at my assigned time. While you were sitting down by the officer's desk, you see a yellow piece of sticky note on the computer with a telephone number and a nickname written on it.

This must be a nickname, who would call themselves Murda? You then tear the sticky note and throw it in the trash can.

In the morning, all inmates get ready for breakfast. They are walking in the pod waiting for the food trays. The inmate that was in your office last night is also a kitchen worker. From the back of the dorm, you hear another inmate yell, "Yo, Murda!" What are we having for breakfast today?

BANG! What's going through your mind?

What would you do in this situation?

You might think there is something going on between the officer and the trustee.

Policy states: At no time are inmates allowed in the officer's quarters, alone with any correctional staff member during the night shift. A supervisor or another staff member must be present. All inmate workers are aware of this policy. Any inmate in violation of this policy will face disciplinary action.

S2: Today is your last day of on the job training in the jail. You observe another Detention Officer being verbally abusive to inmate Davenport in the middle of the lunch room area where everyone can hear him. Inmate Davenport is getting angry at the officer for humiliating him in front of all the other inmates. The other inmates are laughing and pointing their fingers at inmate Davenport.

Suddenly it appears as if inmate Davenport is in a defensive fighting stance and is going to strike the officer with a closed fist. Inmate Davenport is holding a sharp object on his other hand. It appears to be a sharpened pencil. The situation seems to be getting intense.

What would you do?

You would attempt to immediately defuse the situation, by taking the inmate to the side and talk to him. Hopefully you will be the officer that will calm him down. You don't want to make a bad situation worse.

S3: You walk into a pod to relieve an officer for his lunch break. Before the officer goes on his break, you and the officer observe two inmates arguing in the middle of the lunch room. Then you see both inmates getting into a physical confrontation. (Both inmates hitting each other with closed fists).

You are the first one to see it, you immediately yell, break it up! Both inmates comply with your directive. Then, the inmates tell you that the other day, two more inmates were fighting and the other officer let them fight for two minutes and they have proof.

What would you do?

This can go one of two ways:

- Talk directly to the officer who is being Implicated or,

- You can go to an immediate supervisor to discuss the situation.

It might be better to speak to the officer who is being implicated first. Give him/her a chance to fix the situation.

Here I am surrounded by approximately 120 inmates. What's one to do? I take it one day at a time. Do I feel scared? No. I guess it's just me.

Some people say that if you're not scared when you enter an unfamiliar place like jail, you are afraid but it's kept inside. That's not true in my case. I guess I felt that way because of my self-defense training while growing up. I was never afraid of being in front of big crowds. Confidence goes a long way.

I'm not Bruce Lee, rest his soul. But I do know how to handle certain sticky situations. You must stay focused. Show the inmates who is boss. But don't overdo it.

Give them respect. After all, they are human beings just like us.

Some inmates fell on the wrong side of the tracks and are now in the system and need to follow the rules while they are doing their time.

They follow the institution rules, you follow your officer manual to the letter and you should be good.

S4: You're making your regular rounds in your unit. An inmate approaches you and tells you that someone took his Suave Shampoo bottle that he left in the shower, and he thinks he knows who did it.

When you ask him to verify his accusation, he states that the inmate was seen by another officer who worked the unit two nights ago.

What would you do?

You reach out to the other officer to see if the inmate's information is corroborated by the officer. You can ask the inmate, why he didn't take care of the matter when the other officer was there.

You can also make an announcement to the whole unit about the shampoo. That way it won't happen again.

If the inmate wants, he can always buy another shampoo. Keep it in a safe place and no one will think about taking it.

Post orders: Read your post orders thoroughly and understand them. They are made mostly for an assigned location. You should always keep it in a safe place and away from inmates' eyes. If you have any questions always contact your immediate supervisor.

Dorm or Unit Keys: should always be on your person, carried inconspicuously. I always kept mine in my pants pocket on a key holder.

Radio traffic: This is one of my pet peeves. It is always best to keep the radio traffic to a minimum when working in a correctional institution. Don't yell on the radio. Everyone can hear you fine if you speak in a calm and controlled voice.

You never know what's going to happen. If you're making your rounds while the inmates are sleeping, and out of nowhere, someone calls for a radio check in a loud voice, the inmates will blame you for waking them up.

Let's say two inmates are in a fight, there is a medical emergency in a dorm, or worse, hope this never happens, a staff member is down. Keep the lines of communication clear and to the point. Plus, you never know who is listening. If it pertains to work then it is allowed.

In the late 1990's while working at a security company in New York, I noticed they had the latest model two-way Motorola radios.

The frequency on the radios were so high tech, I later found out the police officers in the precinct that was across the street from us could hear everything that we were saying.

Always keep it professional.

Thinking about going to jail can be upsetting. Especially for those who know they are about to do some hard time.

How would your friends and family feel about you going to prison? They must pay your legal fees, which can be expensive. And pay for your phone calls and canteen items.

I have worked with gangsters, pimps, and female hustlers. From disorderly conduct, DWI, failure to appear, rape, possession of controlled substance, child endangerment cases to murder. All were Federal, State and County levels.

There were many people in my life that gave me there input and feedback that finally lead me on the path (friends, family and my girlfriend at the time) to becoming a law enforcement officer.

There were some of my friends I grew up with and spent time with in my adolescent life. Some of them got into trouble and some went on to bigger and better things. I decided back then that a life of crime was not a life for me.

I once observed an inmate tell an officer:

Portate Bien. The Spanish phrase (Portate bien) translates to behave or be good in English. This was a male inmate talking to a female officer. It made me think that the officer had a secret relationship with the inmate.

For an inmate to make such a bold statement to an officer, he had me dumbfounded for a second. Or he made that statement because he liked her.

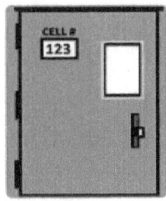

I knew she knew what he was saying because of the way she looked at him when he made that comment. I don't think anything ever happened between them. I guess that was a way of the inmate trying to manipulate the officer. I did not say anything to the officer because she did not know I understood Spanish. She could have stopped him in his track though. Don't you think?

It's always good to stay in shape while you're working in any correctional institute. Exercise regularly but don't overdo it. If you can afford it, take some self-defense classes.

You can research some videos on YouTube as well for free. Practice makes perfect. It will help you in the long run to be alert and learn some techniques just as an extra precautionary measure.

When it comes to self-defense, I can defend myself when approached by anyone in a threatening manner.

I would like to give a big shout out to UFC and MMA fighters. Watching how hard they train is a great way to pick up some good information. Just remember, the best training will always be at your recruit academy training.

S5: You are working in an open dorm and your night shift is almost over. All the inmates are in their assigned bed. Before the other officer relieves you, she makes her first round in the dorm to make sure everything is going well.

Suddenly one of the inmates, who she can't see, because it came from the back area, yells out the female officer's first name. The officer doesn't do anything about it. You heard it, and so did she.

Before you leave your post, you address the inmates and tell them that you will be back tomorrow and that this sort of behavior will not be tolerated.

You tell the officer in question, that before you leave the building you will tell a supervisor about what just occurred. She says its ok; some of the inmates in the dorm know me from when i was in high school. It's been awhile, but they remember my name. I can't do anything about it.

What would you do in this situation? Should you leave it alone since it doesn't bother her? What's going to happen if you tell a supervisor?

S6: You are a correctional supervisor. You get along with all the staff members. There is one officer, who hangs out with you on a regular basis. The officer is like a sister to you.

One day while you and your buddy, were sitting in a restaurant sipping on some wine, she tells you that she's been having a sexual relationship with one of the inmates in one of the dorms, for approximately two years now.

She told you this in confidence. And she wanted you to swear not to tell anyone. What if the inmate received confidential information from her?

What would you do? You're off duty. She told you this in confidence. This is a security issue. It can jeopardize your relationship. Putting you in an uncomfortable position

Should this stay off the record?

Would you keep it a secret? If that's what she's done, could you imagine what else she got away with?

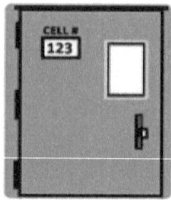

Things to consider if a confrontation should arise: When approaching a confrontation between inmates, do not focus on what brought on the confrontation. Do your best to resolve the situation before it gets worst.

Be professional when talking to an inmate. Don't assume that inmates don't know their rights. Sometimes it's not what you say it's how you say things that can start a riot or defuse a situation.

Personal Matters outside of the work place: Leave your personal matters at the door!

Be willing to step away from those conversations that are of a personal nature. Ignore them.

Some inmates find the simplest ways to get you into these unwanted talks about your life outside the prison walls. Such as, CO what's your favorite car? 90% of the time, it's the car you already drive.

Your marital status is on a need to know basis. Staff could know. Inmates do not need to know if you are married or not. That falls under your personnel information. The less they know about your personal life the better your work day will go. If I had a dollar, for every time an inmate asked me if I was married, I'd be driving a Lexus by now.

There is no reason for you to discuss or show the following in the work place around inmates:

1) The person you slept with last night.

2) The top speed on your Lexus.

3) The highway you took to get to work.

4) Your nationality. Does it matter?

5) The distance it takes you to get to work.

6) Don't show your personal letters. Do you really want them to know who you're writing to?

7) Do you really need to carry your child's picture in front of your uniform shirt pocket? What would you do if your child was a victim of an inmate you knew?

8) Don't leave your car keys lying around on your desk. Inmates observe everything. Like the kind of vehicle, you drive.

9) How you feel about other staff members. Keep it to yourself. Even if they make a comment on one of the staff members.

10) You feel sorry for a certain inmate: A correctional nurse once hugged an inmate because she heard his mother had just passed away. I said to myself, this kind of job is not for her.

11) Do you really have to tell them what supervisor you like the most? Don't talk about your fellow coworkers.

12) What actor/actress your spouse resembles. Here you go again, talking about your spouse. Overhearing a conversation: officer talks to an inmate about his family matters. I guess the inmate was entertained by the officer's family history.

13) The websites you go to when you're at work. Keep it away from their view. How many times in your career has an inmate asked if you could Google something for him?

14) A picture of you and your friends in your civilian clothes. You're asking for it.

15) Don't let inmates know you are on the phone with a family member or show any kind of emotion. They can tell whether you are angry or in a peaceful mood.

This is how they know how their day will go or what buttons they will try to push with you.

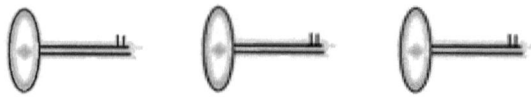

Never give your dorm keys to an inmate.

If you get locked inside a cell and can't get out, call a supervisor or a fellow officer over your radio. You may get written up, but at least you followed protocol.

If you have a computer in your office or your desk, do not use it while the inmates are out and about unless its work related. If you are going to use it, do not go into social media websites.

It can get you into a lot of trouble. Especially, when the inmates know what you are doing. In any case social media is always to be kept outside of the work place.

One day on my scheduled shift, I was relieving an officer from her duties. When she left the office, a couple of inmates were telling me that she wasn't paying much attention to them. I asked them, what they meant by that.

One inmate stated: All she kept doing was looking at the computer all day. Then one inmate told me that the officer I relieved was on Facebook chatting with friends.

I knew they were telling me the truth because when I relieved the officer she had just logged off Facebook. Policy states to stay away from social media while performing your work duties.

Not only do these inmates know what you're doing on the computer, they remember the date and time. When they catch you off guard, they can always tell a supervisor or write a grievance on you for not doing your job. You were being distracted with social media or any other non-job-related matters.

Don't give unauthorized items to an inmate and don't accept any gifts from an inmate.

Don't divulge or share any personal information with or in the presence of any inmates.

Don't personally interact with inmates.

Our motto, always, is being firm, fair and consistent.

Be yourself. Not who they want you to be. Don't be afraid to say no.

Be careful how you answer when an inmate asks you a question. It's not what you say these days that can get you in a jam. It's how you say it.

When speaking to an inmate you can address them as follows. Come over here Sir. Not, you come over here!

An inmate once asked me, if a certain supervisor was married. I replied with I don't know, why? He stated, because he wanted to write a request to her and he wanted to address her the right way. There's a first for everything. I told him to put the rank of the supervisor followed by her name. It will be formal and the best thing to do. Never give out any personal information about a fellow officer or supervisor.

I can go on, but then I won't have any material for my second book.

Some inmates have all day to study you. Do the same in an inconspicuous way.

It's a dangerous profession. We all knew what we signed up for when taking this job. Some inmates have nothing but time on their hands. Some either do their time and get out or do their time and find ways to hurt other inmates or staff members. Unfortunately, this is what we must go through.

Games inmates play. Call you friend, buddy even try to figure out your first name to make it look like you owe them something for them not to tell anyone. This makes them think they can compromise you. Don't take it personally; it's just business on their end.

There are predators and there is prey. A man once asked a group of training cadets; Are you a wolf or are you a sheep dog? A wolf wants prey. A sheep dog is like a leader.

Be a controller not the one being controlled.

Years ago an inmate was talking to me about his case. Before he could go any further I told him that I cannot discuss any legal matters. He continued to state that the evidence was swallowed, as I was calmly walking away doing my rounds.

He said they charged him with destroying evidence. I tried to keep a straight face, but I must admit that was funny. I told him to consult his legal representative.

Don't get involved or give the inmate your input. Whatever you tell an inmate, he will hold you up to. Some never forget what you tell them.

Get to know your inmates. Know what makes them tick. When I was working for a certain prison, an inmate stated to me that she knew what my first name was. I replied with, it doesn't matter if you know my name; you can't do anything with it anyway.

I showed her that I wasn't going to get scared of what she said. Later on, I found out that an officer told her my first name. I did my kind of investigation.

If an inmate wants to get information on you, they will try until they get it. Sometimes you can't trust the people you work with. Sometimes loose officer's lips could sink your ship.

Don't let anything or anyone get to you while working at any prison system.
It's not good for you or your work environment. Staying calm and in control not only makes your day go faster but the inmates won't try to dig for information on you. They know who is confident.

Never get into a shouting match with an inmate. If you do, you lost the battle. He's got you right where he wants you. And, it's not good for business. Calm down and control the situation. Yes, you can do it.

To an inmate you can be a mentor. You are an ear to listen to. You are someone who consoles an inmate. You are a role model. To some, you are a mother and father figure.

While I was working for the state prison system, a good buddy of mine (A fellow Correction Officer) took an inmate out of the unit and started to talk to him in front of me. The officer was consoling the inmate. I saw that the inmate looked at the officer with gratitude.

I remember him telling the inmate, "This place (prison) is not for you." He didn't belong. It's a great feeling to know that he talked to an inmate about him doing better for himself after he gets out of prison.

The inmate told his parents what the officer did for him. A couple of days later, the inmate's parents called the prison to thank the officer for what he has done. You don't get that every day.

An inmate once told me, "I don't like you because of what you do; however, I respect you for the kind of person that you are." You never disrespected us.

S7: Before staff members are given their assignment at your institution, everyone was advised, by the supervisor, not to let a certain officer in the building. It was stated during roll call that this officer was dismissed from her duties, due to her inappropriate behavior with inmates. Everyone knows who the officer is.

While you were making your daily shakedowns in the 2nd floor dorms, you observe a picture of a female hanging on the wall of one of the inmate's cell.

It's a picture of a female in a bikini, on the beach. You observe the picture closely and find that the female officer that was dismissed from your employment is the same female one on that picture.

Since she was dismissed a week ago, you think nothing of it. But this will be on your mind for the rest of your shift.

What would you do?

Would you report it to your immediate supervisor? If you do, you can find out if it has been reported before.

Would you confront the inmate and ask him who the girl on the picture is? He might not want to tell you. Or he might think you want to get to know her.

Would you leave it alone, so that another officer can discover it?

S8: Your assignment for today is the Computer and Monitor room located in the Investigations Office of your facility. As per your post orders, you're supposed to observe everything that is going on in random pods. If you see something out of the ordinary, you are supposed to write it on your observation sheet.

At the end of everyone's shift, the observation sheet should be filled with the institution's Investigations office. Since everything appears normal, you pan in on a female dorm.

It's approximately 2am and all the female inmates should be in their assigned bunks. At approximately 2:15am you see the pod officer, your best bud, going into the janitor's closet. Soon after, you see an inmate going to the janitor's closet and close the door behind her.

It's beginning to look weird considering the inmate should not be in the janitor's closet at that time, and with any officer. Especially with the door closed.

The time now is 3am. You call the officer in question, by radio to check up on him. He's not answering his radio.

Shortly after, you see him coming out of the closet pulling up his pants, and the female inmate right behind him, buttoning her inmate uniform shirt.

Does this look like foul play? What will you put on the observation sheet, since this is your best buddy? Will you let it go? You just put the time and date of scene on the observation sheet before all this occurred. You can't erase it. And it has a file number on it.

How would you handle this situation? You could tell him that you saw what happened and that he should confess to the supervisors immediately or you will tell. Would you give him a chance to explain? It might take time before he does, or even days. So, what's keeping you?

S9 Your assignment for today is the recreation yard. You are happy because tomorrow is your day off. The yard is open and the inmates are playing basketball. It is your responsibility to make sure that no inmates get hurt while playing in the yard.

An inmate steps up to you and states, that he had an argument with another inmate five minutes ago.

But he didn't get into a physical altercation because he respects you and he doesn't want to mess up your day with paperwork. In return, you tell him, "thank you for not fighting."

Your shift is now over and you're going home to your family. You think nothing is going to go wrong because you will be off tomorrow.

When you get back to work, you find that two inmates were fighting in the yard last night. Your supervisor tells you that one of the inmates that were in the fight was on video talking to you in the yard a couple of days ago.

That inmate is in the hospital, and in critical condition. He has two stab wounds and a scratch near his right eye.

What do you think is going to happen, when the chain of command finds out the inmate told you he was about to fight, but because of you, they decided to do it another day? This happens a lot. Most inmates rather break the rules around staff members who they don't respect.

Would you feel guilty?

What will you tell your supervisor now?

S10: You're in the yard with your supervisor. Some of the inmates are playing sports. Some are sitting down by the benches.

A couple of inmates decided to form a circle.

As per your institution rules and regulations, no groups of more than four inmates are allowed to gather in a circle, when in the recreation yard.
You and your supervisor observe that there are approximately 10 inmates gathering in a circle, holding hands and it appears to you, that they are praying.

Your supervisor is telling you to go over there and to check it out. While you approach the inmates, one of them tells you, Get out of here CO! You don't belong here. You immediately tell them to break it up.

You observed one inmate running toward another inmate with an object that looks like a knife. The situation is getting dangerous. While you call for backup, you also observe your supervisor leaving the scene.

Now you are alone with approximately 50 inmates in the yard. One inmate got stabbed and two more are fighting. Backup arrives. But someone is missing.

How do you feel? Are you going to write up your supervisor for leaving the scene? What if he tells you that he left the yard because his radio was not working and he needed another battery? Prepare to make a report.

S11: Today is Christmas Eve. You're approaching the jail parking lot and you're getting ready to go to receiving and discharge. This area is for inmates that are being released from prison.

While going down the stairwell, you see an officer, and a male, who you recognize as an inmate, leaving the release area behind the parking lot.

The officer sees you and tells you that since the inmate doesn't have any money, she is going to give him a ride to the nearest gas station where he will meet his family. You look at her and say, you are crazy! Two minutes after, you get to your post and look up the inmate's information to verify if he was released.

The computer system shows that the inmate in question is still on the system as, "Awaiting Trial". Do not remove from facility! What would you do? Does it look like an escape attempt?

S12: You are working an 11pm to 7am shift. It's approximately 6:45am and you are making your last round before you get relieved from your duties. All inmates are in the day room watching TV.

While making your last round, you observed one inmate tell another inmate that the girl he spoke to last night on the phone will be waiting for his phone call when she gets out of work around 7:05am.

The inmate also mentioned the girl's name, and you think it's one of your coworkers.

When he mentioned her name, they were looking at you like they were caught saying something they shouldn't have.

Staff members are not allowed to have phone conversations with inmates who are incarcerated in the same jail they work in.

What would you do?

S13: You are the dorm officer. Its late night and all inmates appear to be sleeping. An inmate gets up from his bunk, approaches your desk and tells you, that he wants to speak to you and a supervisor in private. You tell him that before he speaks to a supervisor you need to know what the conversation is about.

He states that he has information that can compromise the security of the County jail. You call your supervisor and he immediately responds.

Now that you are all together in a private room, the inmate tells you that another inmate has an employee email, and has been emailing one of your coworkers for quite some time now. The inmate's statement was verified, and found to be truthful. The officer in question was interviewed.

She did tell the truth. For that, she was suspended from her job for 6 months. She kept her job because of pending investigation.

The investigators are putting together a case on the unauthorized communication with an inmate through government equipment. What's wrong with this picture? There are different reasons why staff members get terminated from employment: inappropriate behavior with inmates, bringing contraband into the facility and more.

Working at a prison can put a strain on a person. However, if you love your job, you can handle it. Most people enjoy their job.

I find that some of the officers I have worked with were more stressed at home then at work. A buddy once told me that he felt happy when he was at work. It gave me an indication that something was wrong in the home front, and I was right. He worked a lot of overtime. He hardly spent time at home. He said his wife always fought with him because of money situations. He made it, she takes it.

Don't take your personal life to work.

Take it easy and relax.

Stay positive. Move forward.

Stay focused.

Most inmates that genuinely want to do their time don't want to stir the pot. They just want to go home.

S14: Your friend, Mr. John Doe, who is a registered nurse, just started to work at your detention facility. Nurse Doe is scheduled to distribute medication to the inmates in your pod.

The first inmate to receive his medication identified himself, and told the nurse that he put in a sick call form a while ago, to get his pain medication and he never received it.

Nurse Doe gave the inmate a medical form to fill out. Then you observe Nurse Doe say, ok here you go, take this. The nurse gives the inmate a small plastic see-through bag, with a white grainy substance in it. The inmate immediately left the nurse's location, to avoid questioning from you.

At the time, you didn't think anything of it. However, you felt confused. Should you have asked the nurse about the contents of the plastic bag? The nurse doesn't have to tell you what kind of medication he gave to the inmate. Or else he would be violating some laws.

The next day, a coworker tells you that the same thing happened in his pod, with the same nurse. You are beginning to think this is suspicious activity, and you report it to your supervisor.

A couple of days later, Nurse Doe is in the News. He was suspected of smuggling contraband into a county jail, to inmates, for money. Do you feel like you did justice? You can stop the flow of contraband by doing your job.

To those who go unnoticed, thank you for a job well done.

Leave the medical talk for the medical staff. Ladies and gentlemen: If you have medical experience, don't get involved. That's not your job. You are not part of the medical staff. Should you get the medical staff when needed? Yes! Your opinion might get an inmate hurt on your watch.

Don't tell an inmate he needs a Tylenol when you know he has a sprained ankle. Give the inmate a sick call, call the medical office and have the inmate seen by the medical professionals. Call medical. At least you did your part.

Don't give an inmate any suggestion on any medication to ask for or take for any ailment. Under no circumstances is your input safe here, for yourself or the inmate.

S15: You and a fellow officer are posted in the recreational yard, at a maximum-security prison. When two officers are posted together, in a unit or recreation yard, and one decides to go on break, they must log it in their log book.

It's a very hot day and the inmates are playing sports and some, are sitting on a bench cooling down. Your partner tells you that he is leaving his post because he is thirsty and needs to get a drink of water. You tell him its ok, since you are confident that nothing will happen while he is away for a couple of minutes. Since this sort of thing happens frequently, you don't bother to put your partner's break in your log book.

Ten minutes passes by and you are worried that your partner didn't even call you over the radio to let you know if he's occupied with something else. You call him over the radio, and he's not responding. You wait two more minutes, still no response.

You immediately call your supervisor over the radio to let him know that your partner is missing. Now, every staff member in the facility is calling him over the radio and cannot find him.

Once they check the camera system, they find that your partner was observed talking to an inmate from another location away from the recreational yard.

And it appeared by looking at the camera, that your partner and the inmate were having a verbal discussion which led to a physical altercation.

The last place they were seen together was by the janitor's closet in the hallway. But the inmate was the only one seen coming out of the closet.

When the supervisors went to check the closet, they found the body of your partner, inside a garbage can.

Were any rules broken?
How would you feel if you were the officer who just lost his partner?

S16: Your assignment for today is the Medical Observation unit. You are supposed to do a round every 15 minutes to check up on the inmates who need medical attention. But today, there's only one inmate in your medical observation room.

She can have a flexi pen and paper. Every time you do a round you should make a note of it on your daily log sheet.

It's 2am and the inmate appears to be sleeping.

A couple of minutes later, while making your rounds, you observe the inmate waving goodbye to you from inside her cell. In return, you wave to her without saying a word, and continue with your rounds.

The next time you make your rounds the inmate asks you for a cup of water. You tell her to go back to sleep because she doesn't look like she is thirsty. The inmate goes back to sleep because you told her to.

Fifteen minutes later, the inmate tells you that she needs to speak to a nurse about her medical condition.

You tell her that the nurse is away making her rounds, and that when she comes back, you will relay the message. The inmate says ok to you, but with a sad look on her face. At this time, you are walking back to your desk.

When you make another round, the inmate tells you that she feels tired, thirsty, and dizzy. And that she hasn't had anything to eat today. All she is asking for is a cup of water. You tell her, go to sleep! The nurse is not here! And continue to walk away from her cell.

When the nurse comes back from making her rounds, she asks if everything is ok with the inmate. You tell the nurse that the inmate is sleeping and there is nothing to report.

Your shift is almost over and you are in a hurry to go home. When you approach the inmate's cell, she tells you that she is thirsty, tired and feels dizzy. You tell her that you don't have time for her games. And that you're not giving her anything, because you think she is lying about feeling dizzy.

The inmate immediately looks at you and tells you to go get the nurse because she feels like she's going to faint. You tell her to stop joking, because you know she is faking it.

Now that your relief has arrived, you get ready to go home. You sign out on your time sheet and off you go out the door. You leave without telling anyone about the inmate's condition.

The next day you come to work and observe a sign on the medical unit door. It says, Investigation Do Not Enter. Someone on the other side gets your attention and tells you to come in. When you enter the unit, an investigator looks at you and tells you that he wants to show you something.

He shows you last night's observation sheet with your name on it.

You tell the investigator, you completed all your rounds last night. Is something wrong? The investigator tells you that you are right about the rounds. However, you left out a couple of details.

- You didn't tell the nurse that the inmate needed medical attention.

- You didn't give the inmate a cup of water when she asked for it.

- You were seen on camera waving your hand to her as you were walking by her cell. You dint even stop to talk to her.

- You told her that you didn't have time for her games, then you walked away.

- You also told her that you thought she was lying about her condition.

That's not true, you say. He tells you, since you were the only officer working last night, you are now under investigation.

He tells you, the inmate died last night right after you signed out on your time sheet.

You tell the investigator that you didn't even touch the inmate nor did you give her anything to hurt herself with. The investigator stated, that if you would have given her a cup of water, she wouldn't have been complaining.

Do you have anything to say about this incident? The investigator tells you. How did you know all this happened? You asked. Well, he said. We found a note in her cell. She wrote a statement on that paper and now, it's a legal document.

The inmate wrote everything on a piece of paper. The time she asked for water, and who she asked. The video corroborates with what she said you did, and the time it happened.

The inmate died of a heart attack. Plus, the medical examiner found that she had signs of dehydration.

You failed on so many levels. Get ready to answer a lot of questions. Don't ignore the warning signs.

Treat all inmates with respect. Remember, they can't wear your uniform. But, you can wear theirs.

S17: Your shift is almost over. You just made your last round and you're finishing your paperwork. While you are at your desk, you notice that all the inmates are quiet.

It looks weird to you because its 8am and the inmates are usually watching TV at this time. You hear a couple of inmates arguing in the back of the unit, but you can't see them from your desk.

While you walk to the back, you observe two inmates fighting near a water fountain. One inmate has a bloody nose.

You tell them to break it up before you deploy your OC spray. You pick up your radio to call for backup.

While you pick up your radio, your supervisor immediately walks in the unit, tells you not to call it over the radio, and orders the two inmates to stop fighting. Both inmates comply with the direct order.

Your supervisor immediately tells the inmates to go back to their bunks, and forget everything ever happened. Both inmates quietly go back without hesitation.

He also tells them that it is time for the officers to go home and he doesn't want to see this happen again.

You ask the supervisor if you should make an incident report on what happened. He tells you not to make it because it was handled by him. I don't think the inmates will fight again, the supervisor says.

Your supervisor gives you a direct order not to tell anyone about the fight. He is not interested in doing paperwork before he goes home.

You feel guilty about not telling anyone. But, you want to go home on time. You don't want to be written up for not following your supervisor's orders.

What do you think will happen to you for not reporting the fight? After all, you did follow orders.

Do you think the supervisor was right in what he did? The inmate with the bloody nose probably needed medical attention.

The inmates in that unit probably think they can get away with doing just about anything.

I would probably separate them. Reassign them to different units. And have them on file as, "Do Not House in Same Unit."

Do you feel hopeless? Who would you count on for back-up?

S18: Your assignment for today is the computer room. Your job is to monitor inmate phone conversations and you do this on a regular basis.

Policy states, Inmates are not allowed to participate in three-way phone calls. If the investigating officer encounters the three-way, he/she must report it immediately to the supervisor of the day.

You are well known by the inmates. You would recognize most inmates' voice if you hear them on the phone.

The first call you are monitoring is of two inmates who are residents of the same facility.

Since they can't call each other, how could this have happened?

Inmate #1 called his mother from his unit phone at approximately 3pm. His mother answered the phone, continues a five-minute conversation with him, and then you hear someone else joining the conversation. Suddenly it sounds like a three-way conversation.

You recognize the voice of the third person. It sounds like inmate #2, one of the female inmates that you speak to on a regular basis.

By listening a little closer to the details of the conversation, you are sure that inmate #2 is also calling inmate #1's mother.

While you monitor the inmates, you find that they are having a normal conversation.

However, Inmate #1 is in a male dorm, and inmate #2 is in a female dorm.
Both inmates are married and have been in prison for more than two years now.

Since you know both inmates well, and they never give you any problems, you feel like what they did was not a violation.

You know that inmates are not allowed to make three-way phone calls. Why would you let this go? They don't get a pass just because you know them.

The conversation could have been about a HIT on one of the other inmates or, a staff member.

This kind of behavior must be reported to the Investigations Department. Would you report it?

Both inmates will have their telephone privileges taken away for 45 days or more. Who knows how many times this has happened.

S19: You and your supervisor are getting ready to go on a hospital trip, which is one hour away. Before leaving the facility, you tell the inmate that he will be handcuffed in the front since he's the only one going to the hospital. He will also need leg irons.

Your supervisor tells the inmate that due to policy, he has no time to use the restroom on the way to the hospital. The inmate had an opportunity to use the restroom before leaving the facility.

Thirty minutes into the trip, the inmate tells you he needs to use the restroom. You tell him that he was warned before leaving the facility. No bathroom breaks on the way to the hospital.

The inmate tells you that he really needs to go, and that if you don't stop, he will have an accident in the transport van.

Your supervisor is starting to feel sorry for the inmate. So, he tells you to please stop the van so the inmate can use the restroom, at the nearest gas station. You tell your supervisor he is going against policy.

He says, no one will know. Anyway, all he wants is to do number one.

You tell him, no! We're almost at the hospital! Your supervisor now tells you that he must go. Both of you know that you must wait till you get to the hospital.

Since your supervisor gave you a direct order, you decide to stop the van, while he uses the restroom in the nearest gas station.

When your supervisor got back to the van, he took the inmate's handcuffs off. Took his shackles off, and told him to stay with him while they both walk to the rest room.

Five minutes later, your supervisor comes back to the van by himself. He tells you that the inmate had a little accident in the bathroom, so he decided to leave him alone since there is no one else in the gas station.

The supervisor immediately goes back into the gas station and comes right back to the van, and asks you if you are playing games with him. No, you say. Why? He tells you that he didn't see the inmate at the gas station and he thinks he escaped.

The inmate is calmly walking toward the van, and says, hey guys, let's go. "Whereabouts do you come from?" You ask. We were looking for you. He replied with, I was talking to some girl in the gas station.

The supervisor, without hesitation, quickly puts the handcuffs and leg irons on the inmate. When you get to the hospital, the supervisor tells you not to do a report on what just happened.

This can cost both of us our jobs. So, please don't mention it to anyone. The supervisor says. As far as the inmate is concerned, he will not say anything since he relieved himself in the gas station's bathroom, and he feels satisfied.

Who is the driver? Do you think the supervisor could have used better judgment?

Do you think the inmate is going to keep quiet about what happened? Someone, sooner or later will find out.

S20: You are assigned to a male Special Housing Unit, located in a maximum-security Prison. You have only ten inmates locked-up in your unit.

A couple of them are there because of Protective Custody issues. Most of them are there for fighting with another inmate.

You get along with all of them and you don't have any current issues.

During your lunch break, you decide to eat in your unit, but in an area where the inmates can't see you.

A female officer walks into your unit to relieve you. While she conducts her rounds, the inmates in your unit are suddenly making cat calls and calling her sexy.

While eating your lunch, you observe the female officer to see how she reacts to those comments.

You can tell that she felt uncomfortable, and she's about to say something to the inmates.

The officer tells the inmates, shut the hell up if you know what's good for you! The inmates get riled-up and start booing her. You make an announcement to the inmates to please calm down, and be quiet while the officer makes her rounds.

One inmate says, (in a loud voice) She's no good to us! Every time she comes in here she has a nasty attitude. The female officer responds with, shut up!

The only reason you are in here, is because you are a child molester. Suddenly, all the inmates started to bang on the cell doors.

You pull the officer to the side and ask her, why did she say that? She tells you that they deserve what she said.

They don't know how to speak to a lady! Then you tell her that she shouldn't have said that because now, the inmates know why he is in here for.

Did the female officer react in a calm and professional manner?

The inmate the female officer was talking about can now make a formal complaint about the female officer for saying what he was in Protective Custody for.

S21: Its Monday morning. The inmates are getting ready to go to court. Some of the inmates are going to be transported to the nearest hospital for a medical appointment.

Inmate Carter, who is not scheduled to go to court or a medical appointment, asks if you knew who was going to the hospital, because he has a brother who is in another pod who is scheduled to go on a hospital trip.

You tell inmate Carter, that you cannot give out any information about other inmates.

Inmate Carter then tells you that he spoke to his mother on the phone. She told him that his brother is scheduled to go to the hospital today.

All he wants to know is the time his brother's appointment is scheduled for.

You advise him that if he insists on asking that question again, he will go on lockdown.

Inmate Carter tells you that other officers always give him any information he asks for. And that you are the only one who doesn't do it.

You are starting to feel sorry for inmate Carter. And he can see it on your face.

While you talk to inmate Carter, you calmly put the transportation sheet down on your desk so he can see it. How many times have you seen this happen?

Inmate Carter looks down at the sheet, gives you a smile, and then walks away.

The next day you go to work. Your supervisor tells everyone during roll call, that an inmate was killed yesterday in route to the hospital emergency room.

The transportation officer was not hurt. Read the investigative report.

Investigative Report: While the transportation officer was entering the emergency room with the inmate, an unknown male approached the officer and the inmate that was being transported.

The unknown male pulled out a knife and stabbed the inmate in the chest and stomach area several times.

The Transportation officer tried to subdue the suspect but the suspect got away. He couldn't leave the injured inmate alone.

The inmate died a couple of minutes after being stabbed because he lost a lot of blood.

The transportation officer did his job by trying to protect the inmate. It will be a day he will never forget.

The next day, after an investigation was done, it was concluded that the inmate that was being transported was a victim of a HIT.

Inmate Carter hired a professional killer to get rid of the inmate that was being transported to the hospital.

Two months ago, the deceased inmate testified in court against inmate Carter. Inmate Carter was part of a drug cartel from Mexico

You gave confidential information about another inmate to inmate Carter. Even though you didn't tell him, it was in your possession and in plain view.
Your intentions were for inmate Carter to see it.

Whether it was inmate Carter's brother or not, you made a big mistake. Now, you have to pay for what you did.

If inmate Carter wanted, he could give you up in an instance. When the investigation is over and they find out you had something to do with the incident, they might think you were an accessory to murder.

What do think? You had a part in this. What do you think the rest of your fellow officers think about you now?

What you did was a breach of security.

When you give out this kind of information, you are jeopardizing the safety of the Transportation officer, as well as the inmate he/she is transporting.

S22: A female officer is assigned to a male dorm. You, a male officer, is about to relieve her for lunch. Before she leaves the unit, she tells you that she is going to leave the computer on, with her personal stuff on it, since she trusts you with her business.

When she leaves the dorm, inmate Rivera, approaches you and states that he wants to speak to you in private, after count time. You tell him that you will open his cell door before everyone else.

A couple of minutes later, you get ready for the afternoon count. All the inmates are in their cells. After the count is over all inmates are to be locked in their cells for another fifteen minutes.

The only inmate you let out now is Rivera. He tells you that the officer you relieved for lunch was the spouse of one the inmates in the unit. He also tells you to check the history on the computer, to show you what he was talking about. Inmate Rivera says that the other inmates are always talking about her. That's how he knew that was his ex-wife.

When you look at the computer's history, you find a picture of the female officer hugging one of the inmates from the unit. According to the time-stamp on the picture, it shows the picture was taken one year ago.

Your facility's policy states, you are not allowed to be assigned to a unit where you and an inmate were once in a relationship. Inmate Rivera tells you that the inmate on the picture is the ex-husband of the officer you relieved.

Inmate Rivera tells you that the officer also gives her ex-husband extra food for breakfast.

The other inmates won't say anything because she is a good officer and she treats the inmates with respect.

You take this information seriously and tell inmate Rivera, "thank you for the information." While inmate Rivera walks away, he states that if you want, he will fill out a statement to verify what he told you.

Would you inform the officer of what inmate Rivera said about her?

This could damage her reputation as a good officer. However, she failed to report that her ex-husband is an inmate in her unit.

S23: You and your wife are both employed as Correctional officers. You've been together for more than five years now and the relationship is great.

You both work at the same facility and on the same shift. However, you are not allowed to work in the same unit together.

One morning, on the drive to work, you receive a phone call from your supervisor, telling you that you are going to be posted in the Worker unit because another officer called in sick.

Your wife tells you that the Worker unit is her favorite. You tell her that you also like that unit since you get along with those inmates and you've known them for at least two years now.

The inmates in the worker unit (Janitor and sanitation crew) are responsible for the cleaning and trash detail for your facility.

While you prepare your paperwork, Inmate Johnson walks up to your desk and asks a question you never heard from an inmate before.

Inmate Johnson tries to remain as inconspicuous as possible so that no other inmate would hear him talking to you.

Johnson: CO, do you trust your wife?

You: If you ask me that question again, you will go on Lockdown!

Johnson: I'm sorry. It's that I must tell you something, because you are a good CO and I don't want to keep this a secret anymore.

You: Johnson, spill it already!

Johnson: The other day your wife was the unit officer. She took inmate Rivera to clean up a stain that was in the unit across from us. That unit is closed for renovation.

You: So, what's the problem? Johnson, what are you insinuating?

Johnson: Inmate Rivera told me that your wife and he went to the closet and had sex.

He also informed me that your wife told him you called in sick, that same day. Check your schedule to see if that was true.

You: You know that most inmates will say anything about an attractive female officer.

Johnson: CO! Please, be careful. Inmate Rivera told me this happened six months ago. He also told me he has HIV. Haven't you noticed that the nurse only comes in here to see him? He's taking Virus medication.

Johnson: You better get checked. But please keep this between you and me.

You: The allegation you just made is very serious. I must look into this matter. Keep your mouth shut until I tell you otherwise!

Johnson: Ok. I won't say a word.

A couple of days later, on your day off, you go to the hospital to get checked. Your wife is not aware of you going to the hospital.

The doctor tells you that you have a virus in your body but can't tell what it is.

He would have to send your blood test and paperwork to a specialist to confirm his diagnosis.

Three days later.

The test results are in. This time, the doctor calls your job to tell you he wants to see you immediately. He cannot discuss the results on the phone.

When you see the doctor, he tells you that you tested positive for HIV, and that prompt medical care is the best way to stay healthy.

The doctor advised you to tell your wife about your situation and to have her tested as well.

When you confronted your wife about what inmate Johnson stated, she confessed to the sexual encounter with inmate Rivera.

What now? How do you feel?

Inmate Johnson was serving a five-year sentence for drug charges. After the investigation was concluded, all charges were dropped from the Prosecutor's office. He only served two of the five.

If it weren't for inmate Johnson, you wouldn't have known about your wife's encounter with inmate Rivera.

The Judge that handled Inmate Rivera's case gave him an extra five years for having sexual contact with a Jail official.

Your wife was sentenced to fifteen years in prison. According to the charges, she admitted to having sexual contact with inmate Rivera.

She was booked on two counts of sexual misconduct with an offender.

After the internal investigation was concluded, it was determined that your wife was also in violation of another Jail Rule: Communicating with inmate Rivera via cell phone when she was not working at the jail.

Inmate Rivera phone records show he called her more than 5 times a week, while all this was happening.

Approximately, six months' worth of phone calls. And she also deposited funds in his inmate account, in return for his silence.

How would you handle this situation?

Is your job and health on the line?

S24: You and another officer, who have been working together for a long time now, are going on a hospital trip to pick up an inmate who has an escape history. He is a known drug dealer and has a lot of money on the outside.

Before you go to the hospital, your supervisor gives you a History Data Sheet on the inmate. The history sheet states that the inmate has a history of manipulating transportation officers in doing what he asked for.

On one occasion, he talked an officer into smuggling cigarettes into the correctional facility. He had a supervisor bring him extra pencils to his unit, only for him to use. That looks like favoritism. He once convinced a female officer to give him her Social Media ID name, so that when he gets out of prison, they can communicate and possibly get together.

When you arrive at the hospital emergency room, you see him lying on his bed. He tells both of you that he needs to let his family know he is in the hospital. You tell him that because of policy and procedure, he is not allowed to communicate with anyone from the outside while he is in the hospital.

The inmate tells you that if you do this for him he will have someone deliver two thousand dollars to you tomorrow morning.

You decline and tell him that is not going to happen.

An hour goes by and you feel hungry. You tell your partner that you are going to step out for a couple of minutes while you get something to eat.

Your partner stays with the inmate, while you leave the hospital room. When you go back to the room, you observe the inmate talking to someone on a cellphone. You tell your partner that he knows that is not right of him to let this sort of thing happen.

Your partner tells you that the inmate just wanted to call his mother. You tell him that you don't like what you are seeing. And that you are going to report this to your supervisor.

What could be the punishment for this kind of behavior? The inmate could be calling someone to help him escape from the hospital.

What would have happened if you agree with your partner's behavior?

S25: You are working an eight-hour night shift. Your assignment for today is the Special Housing Unit, where all the inmates in that unit are not allowed to walk freely.

They are locked-up in their cell 24 hours a day. During the 24 hours, they only get one hour of recreation time.

During your first round, an inmate asks you for the time. You tell him its 1:20am. The next round he asks for the time again. You tell him that its 2:20am.

On your third round, he asks you again for the time. You tell him its 3:20am.

If this continues all night, the inmate can note the times you do your rounds. It can give him enough time to do what he wants to do:

Plan an escape.

Send a kite (written request for something) to other inmates in the unit, or flood his cell.

He can also plan to talk to other inmates in the unit when you're not making your rounds.

Would you ask the inmate why he asked for the time every time you passed by? They're not going anywhere.

It's not like he should make a phone call. An inmate once told me: When I see that you passed by me four times, that's how I know two hours has gone by.

S26: You are working in a female dorm. The inmates see you as a good officer and one they can trust. They all get along with you because they have known you for almost three years now.

Mr. Foster, a Correctional Counselor, supervises the female inmate workers in your unit, and handles their payroll.

When Mr. Foster is in his office, he usually calls certain inmates into his office to discuss their finances, jail status and their evaluations. At approximately 3pm, Mr. Foster calls you on the phone and tells you that he needs to see inmate J. Lopez. She is one of your cleaning and sanitation inmates.

While inmate Lopez goes to the counselor's office, she tells you to please take a note of how long she is gone from your unit. You reply with, I always do. I keep a record of when you leave the unit and when you get back.

She smiles at you and leaves to the counselor's office.

A couple of inmates walk up to your office. While you are sitting on your desk, they tell you that you better watch Mr. Foster because what he is doing is not right.

You ask the inmates to speak freely. What are you talking about? You ask. While the inmates are talking to you, you look at your clock and you notice that it's been two hours since you last saw inmate Lopez.

The inmates in your office hear you mumble, what is taking Lopez so long?

At 5:10pm Inmate Lopez walks into your office with tears on her eyes. She closes the door behind her and tells you that she would like to report a rape.

You observe the two inmates that are in your office immediately and quietly stepping out of your office, as they tell Inmate Lopez that this will be the last time this happens.

You immediately call your supervisor while giving inmate Lopez a witness statement forms to fill out. You tell her that you want her to write everything she witnessed.

She states that the rape occurred in Mr. Foster's office. And that she, is the victim.

Mr. Foster calls your office. He tells you that inmate Lopez is going to make a false accusation against him. And that she told him she would do it unless she gets a raise from her job.

You quickly inform Mr. Foster that the inmate is in your office and she is waiting to see your supervisor. He hangs up. Then he appears in front of your office door, while inmate Lopez is in your office.

You tell him that his presence is not wanted at this moment due to the nature of the incident. Mr. Foster quietly leaves your office and heads back to his assigned area. What's next? The investigation is about to commence.

You have a lot of paperwork to do. And most likely, you will have to go to court. Stick to the facts. No one wants you to be a hero. Just be honest in what you do and everything will fall into place.

S27: You and your buddies are on your lunch break. From time to time you guys get together and share stories about what happened in the past with certain inmates.

Today one of your co-worker's states that yesterday he observed two inmates fighting in the shower area.

There is no video footage of the fight because the cameras are not pointed in that direction, due to privacy issues. He stated that both inmates told him they didn't want to go to the Special Housing Unit, where they hold inmates on disciplinary charges.
The officer didn't report the fight to his supervisor, because he thought it was a fair fight. However, he made a comment on one of the inmates.

He said one of the inmates had a bloody nose, and a black eye. After the fight was over, the inmate went to bed like if nothing ever happened.

The inmate covered himself with his blanket and stood in bed until the officer's shift was over. What you didn't know, is that one of the officers in the break room just got promoted to Sergeant.

Would you keep this to yourself? You could talk the officer into telling a supervisor. On the other hand, he might say that you should mind your own business.

Sooner or later someone is going to tell what the officer observed.

What would you have done in this situation?

The inmates that were in a fight might not say anything. However, one or more inmates might tell another officer or a supervisor what they witnessed.

The officer that didn't report the fight might get fired, suspended or even brought up with charges from the inmates' family, for letting this kind of incident happen.

Inmates, who see this kind of behavior from correctional staff, cannot trust an officer. They might think he's corrupt, crazy, or just someone who likes to see inmates getting into fights.

S28: You and your partner are assigned to work at a Correctional Mental Institution for female inmates. The facility is very old and has no video surveillance cameras.

The unit you are in only holds ten female inmates. They are assigned separate cells to keep them from hurting each other. And are designed in a way where an inmate can't see another inmate.

Its 11pm, and you're getting ready to turn the lights off to all the cells in your unit. The only lights that stay on are the night lights in the cells.

While you yell, Lights Out! The inmates get ready to go to sleep.

You and your partner always take turns in making the rounds. The first round is yours. Because of the size of the unit, it usually takes approximately five minutes to complete a round.

You finished your first round and everything appears normal. All inmates are in their bunk and it appears that they are sleeping.

Your partner starts making his rounds. But before he leaves, he tells you that after he finishes his rounds, he will go to the cafeteria to get a bite to eat. You reply with, ok.

All rounds are made for you and your partner and it's almost time to go home from a hard day's work.

The next day, when you get back to work, your supervisor pulls you to the side to ask you a question.

Did you know, that one of the females in the mental unit stated that an officer raped her last night?

You tell your supervisor that you and your partner made rounds all night and nothing out of the ordinary happened. All our rounds are noted on the log book.

You think to yourself, what could have happened last night?

You find out that your partner called in sick tonight. But you want to get to the bottom of this. You never had any issues while you were working in the institution.

During your tour of duty, you find out that the inmate stated to investigators, that her rapist had a tattoo of a snake on his chest area.

All officers that were scheduled to work that night had to report to the Warden's office, one at a time, for questioning.

You get cleared, and noted as a non-suspect.

Your partner is called to come in to the institution, as soon as possible. When your partner gets to the institution, the Warden tells him to open his shirt to see if he has any tattoos on his chest.

This is done in the presence of an investigator and two other correctional staff.

Your partner has a tattoo of a snake on his chest area. He confessed to having relations with the inmate on the night in question. He also said that the inmate gave him consent.

As per policy, there is zero tolerance toward all forms of sexual activity in the prison.

Correctional staff members are not allowed to have intimate relationships with inmates who are incarcerated in the facility where they work.

Policy also states: Inmates can never agree to have sexual activity with staff members. Any sexual activity between a staff member and an inmate is illegal.

Your partner is facing charges, and the inmate is currently in protective custody.

The inmate was asked by investigators if she voluntarily had sex with your partner. She stated that she would never give officers consent to do anything to her body.

She is now filling for a civil rights case against the officer and the prison.

If your partner is found guilty, he can be convicted of rape and forcible sodomy. Is it worth losing your job for that kind of behavior?

Do you see what you must go through; just because your fellow officer did something he wasn't supposed to do?

These things happen all the time. Be careful, stay focused and stay safe.

S29: A male officer is assigned to a female unit. He gets along with all of them since he's known them for almost 3 years now.

One night while the inmates are sleeping, one of the females approaches his office. She hands him a magazine, and tells him to read it and pay attention to the middle of the magazine.

She then walks away and heads back to her assigned bed.

While opening the magazine to the mid-section, he discovers that her name and cell phone number is printed on a little section in one of the pages.

He knows this is wrong; however, she is being released from prison tomorrow. And he doesn't think it would be wise to reprimand her because she is a good inmate.

While making his rounds he observed that same inmate drinking water from the fountain near his office. He tells her that he will give the magazine back to her. And thank you, but, no thank you.

She smiles and says, you're welcome, hopefully if we see each other in the streets one day we can hook up.

He tells her, you never know.

Do you think the officer is giving the inmate hope that if they see each other one day they might hook up? Would you reprimand the inmate for trying to compromise you?

S30: Your assignment for today is to relieve certain officers for their lunch break. Your first break is a female officer in a male processing unit.

While you wait for the unit door to open, you observe through the glass window on the door, an inmate giving a piece of paper to the officer. It appears that he was giving the officer an inmate request form.

The officer places the form on her desk and in front of the staff computer. The inmate then walks away.

While entering the unit, the officer tells you that she is going to the lady's room before she goes on her break.

While she walks away, you look at the piece of paper the inmate gave her. The paper had his full name and an address on it. It also reads, "Meet me tomorrow at the hotel"

While the officer is still in the rest room, you look up the inmate's name, on the prison system, and then find out the inmate is being released from the prison in one hour.

The officer returns from her bathroom break.

You tell her that you observed an inmate give her a note, she read it, and then placed it on the desk.

She tells you that it's none of your business what kind of papers she has laying around on her desk. It's her unit. And she can do whatever she wants with it.

You tell her that you're going to tell your supervisor about this. I don't care! She says.

When you bring up the incident to your Supervisor, he tells you that he knows what's going on because the female officer told him.

Your supervisor also tells you that the female officer is leaving the job sometime this week because she found another job. So, he doesn't think that he should write her up for that.

Would you feel like no one cares about incidents like this? Some supervisors let things go without thinking about the consequences. Sometimes you are going to feel helpless and must take matters to another level.

S31: Today is News Year's Eve. You are working in the Receiving and Discharge area of a prison. Your job assignment is to take the newly admitted inmates to a search cell, where they are given a full body pat down to find contraband, if any.

Then escort the inmate to his/her next destination. You escort an inmate to the Dress-out room, where they get their prison clothes, and then their property goes to a locked room for safe-keeping.

Before any inmate goes to their assigned unit, they must be visually strip searched. You assume that when the inmate first came into the prison the first officer he saw made a thorough search of the inmate.

During the 2nd stage of the process, while patting down the inmate near the waist area, you find a small plastic bag with a white powdery substance that appears to be cocaine. When you ask the inmate about the contraband, he tells you that the first officer that searched him saw it and didn't do anything about it.

Through further investigation, by video surveillance, it was found that the first officer did in fact let the contraband go through.

Don't cut any corners. What would have happened if it was a knife, a firearm or a syringe in the inmate's possession? The inmate could have been readily capable of causing death or other serious physical injury to anyone who gets in his way.

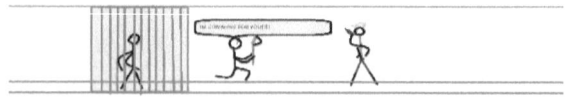

S32: Today is your first day of training in a Correctional facility. You and Officer Jones, your training officer, are assigned to the mail room. Your objective is to inspect outgoing inmate mail for possible contraband. So far you like what you see because it looks like an easy job. While inspecting the outgoing mail, you observed that an inmate wrote a letter to his girlfriend.

The letter stated that he wanted his girlfriend to take care of the business they were talking about on the phone last night. After further investigation, while monitoring the phone conversations, it was found that the inmate wanted to punish an officer for embarrassing him in one of the units.

Officer Jones knows who this officer is. He mentioned to you that the officer is no good and he doesn't like him either. He tells you not to mention anything you have heard or read on the letter written to the inmate's girlfriend.

Put it in the outgoing mail box, Officer Jones says. The officer deserves to get what's coming to him. No one likes him. Not even the inmates.

You tell him, yes, but it's not right that this officer is not made aware of what is going on. He can get seriously hurt. Other officers, can also get caught in the middle.

The prison investigations unit must be aware of the phone calls and the letter written to the inmate's girlfriend. If you don't report it, you are just as guilty as the one telling you not to. Inmate Johnson, hit on another officer your partner doesn't like. Doesn't tell him anything about inform him about the possible hit on the other officer.

Have you ever been in a situation where you wanted to help someone, and then another person comes along and tells you not to?

S33: You are off duty. However, you are working at your part time job, which has nothing to do with corrections.

You and your co-workers are in the staff lounge. On your break, one of your co-workers wants you to talk about the stories you have about your regular job.

You mentioned that you observed an inmate trying to hurt himself by strangulation.

You did the right thing by calling for medical assistance and back up. You told your co-worker the inmate's name, description, and the hospital he was escorted to.

While describing the inmate to your co-worker, it was mentioned that the inmate died in the hospital and that you are happy it didn't happen at your facility. You were also joking about the inmate's sexual preference.

A couple of hours later your co-worker tells you that he has a family member who fits the description of that inmate.

He tells you that he just got off the phone with his mother. She stated to him that the inmate in question was his brother.

You just let the cat out of the bag. The nature of the incident that happened at the prison is very sensitive.

How are you going to fix this situation? You mentioned the inmate's name, and then you made fun of him to his brother.

Your intentions might have been innocent but now, it can cost you your job. Be on guard even when you're off duty.

S34: A couple of days ago, before leaving the correctional facility, Officer Larry took his uniform shirt off in the parking lot so he won't be seen driving home in uniform. H He is left with a dark undershirt. He stood with a dark undershirt.

The parking lot faces the female unit windows. The inmates don't mind seeing the officers taking their shirts off because that's their kind of entertainment. However, it was stated in line-up that as of today, no officer should be taking their shirts off in the parking lot, due to the female inmates yelling out the window when officers leave the facility. Those, who disobey this rule, will face disciplinary action.

You just finished your shift and you are walking to the parking lot with Officer Larry.

He decides to take his shirt off, even though everyone was told not to get undressed in the parking lot. This time he takes off his uniform shirt and the undershirt.

The scene created a disturbance in the female unit because the inmates wanted to see him take his shirt off. Only the inmates that were by the windows saw him.

The officer from the female unit told your supervisor that two female inmates were fighting in the unit because they couldn't see Officer Larry in the parking lot. They were blocked from seeing Officer Larry by other female inmates.

Officer Larry is now suspended from his employment for one week, for disobeying a facility rule, and creating disturbance.

Since you were a witness to him being in the parking lot, when he took off his shirt, you are now required to write a witness statement.

It doesn't look good when your co-worker should write a witness statement on you. Could you have told Officer Larry not to take his shirt off before leaving the building? You could have talked him out of it.

Do not tolerate this kind of behavior from staff members.

S35: While conducting your rounds, you overhear inmate Bobby talking to the other inmates near the dining tables. He mentioned that he is the owner of 123 Construction Company. And that he has a lot of employees under his command. You don't think anything of it because you hear inmates talking about certain things all the time.

On your second round, you overhear inmate Bobby (A well-known gangster), say that an officer who works with you is a part-time worker of his.

According to policy, you are not allowed to associate with anyone who is incarcerated in the prison that you work for. Unless, its family. You immediately report what you heard to the Prison Investigations Department. The head investigator tells you that he is aware of what kind of job the officer was into.

But he never knew who exactly he was working for.

The officer that works construction, on a part-time basis, never revealed that he was working for someone who was incarcerated in the same prison where he works. This can be a trust issue.

Would you report what the inmate said without speaking to the officer first? The officer might not have known that his boss got arrested.

S36: You and another officer are assigned to a female medical unit. Both of you will take turns in making the rounds because one officer must stay by the desk at all times.

You decide to take the rover patrol, while your partner stays by the desk area.

You just finished your first round so you decide to hang around the desk area with your partner. While you approach the desk, your partner tells you that he feels lazy today and he's not doing much work.

Your partner says, "If one of these inmates come up to me and asks for the nurse, I will make believe I'm calling the nurse so they will think she's on her way."

Inmate Garcia approaches your desk and states that she needs medical attention, because she has a head ache and she is feeling suicidal.

Your partner tells her that he will call the nurse. He also tells her to go back to her cell so she can relax. Wait till the nurse gets here, he says. While picking up the phone he makes believe he's talking to the nurse.

Inmate Garcia slowly walks away from the desk area and says, "I'm going to kill myself."

Your partner disregards what the inmate just said. Since you heard what she stated, you tell your partner to call the nurse. Your partner tells you that she is faking it because that's what she always says to get attention.

You take it upon yourself to call the nurse several times, but the line is busy.

Inmate Garcia is now in her cell. You start making your rounds, but your first stop is her cell area. When you arrive at her cell, you observe a blanket tied to her bedpost and the other end of the blanket is tied to her neck.

You immediately call for a medical emergency and backup on the radio.

Your partner is doing nothing to help. And all this is caught on the video surveillance camera. He is sitting by the desk with his arms crossed.

When the nurse and correctional staff arrive, inmate Garcia tells everyone that she told you and your partner that she felt suicidal, and that she also said she felt like dying.

Your supervisor checks your log books and it appears that you didn't enter any information about this inmate on the log book.

Who would be responsible if this inmate would have died? What about your partner? Stick to the facts. You don't want a lawsuit on your hands.

S37: You are a male officer in a female unit, and it's after midnight. All the inmates are supposed to be sleeping on their bunks.

Before the inmates went to sleep you made an announcement, that after the lights go out, all inmates are to remain on their bunks, unless they are going to the bathroom or to drink water.

When you make your first round, everything appears normal and all the inmates appear to be sleeping.

Its 2am. You are on your next round and you notice that an inmate is missing, because you don't see her on her bunk. You immediately check the shower and the bathroom area. No sign of the inmate. At this time, you are worried because you can't find her.

You suddenly go back to your desk and rewind the tape from the video surveillance machine in your unit. The video shows the inmate sneaking to the back of the unit (a well-known blind spot) where she sits down on the floor to talk to another inmate.

Do you give her a warning or do you call for a lock down procedure? What directive did you give the inmates before they went to sleep? What if, she was really missing?

S38: When a family member calls the prison to deliver a (Death in the Family) message to an inmate, it is treated as sensitive information.

Officer Nieves is the Special Housing Unit officer, where inmates are locked in their cell all day and can only come out when they receive their daily one-hour break for recreation or to make telephone calls.

Officer Nieves received a phone call from his supervisor telling him that a family member of inmate Johnson called to say that his mother just died.

Inmate Johnson is known as being very sensitive to certain comments.

Inmate Johnson is two weeks away from being paroled. When inmate Johnson receives this information, it can go a couple of ways:

1) He's going to break down and cry in front of you.

2) He's going to want to start a fight with another inmate, or an officer to relieve some stress.

3) Or he might think about hurting himself.

Inmate Johnson is to immediately call his home and speak to his father. Inmate Johnson is allowed a free phone call. The telephone number of inmate Johnson's father, was given to Officer Nieves, to give to inmate Johnson.

Officer Nieves informs inmate Johnson twelve hours after he received the information. When inmate Johnson called his father, he told him that he just received the message about his mother passing away.

Inmate Johnson is angry and might want to hurt Officer Nieves for not giving him the information sooner. His father will probably want to file a complaint against the prison and the officer that relayed the message.

What could officer Nieves have done to change this situation? Was he right in taking his time with this kind of sensitive information?

S39: Officer Nash is known to be a prankster. One day while receiving a new inmate in his unit, he asked the inmate if he could do him a favor. The inmate told him that he would do it if he gets an extra breakfast tray in the morning.

Officer Nash responded with, ok, you got it. The inmate is a known Spanish gang member. But, Officer Nash doesn't know which gang the inmate is affiliated with. Officer Nash wanted the inmate to go to the dining hall and make believe he was going to steal another inmate's lunch tray. Officer Nash can't believe this is happening. He is happy and giggling with joy.

While the inmate is getting ready to steal another inmate's lunch tray, the officer's office phone rings. Officer Nash leaves the area and heads to his office.

Five minutes later, Officer Nash goes back to the dining hall and sees the new inmate with a black eye and a cut lip.

The inmate that cut the new inmate on the lip and gave him a black eye is a rival gang member. He wasn't supposed to be in that unit in the first place. The bruised inmate was quickly rehoused to another unit for his safety.

This could be a classification problem. However, Officer Nash is under investigation for telling an inmate to steal another inmate's lunch tray. The inmate will probably tell his side of the story when the investigation process begins.

The inmate could have been killed. Do you think Officer Nash should be disciplined?

S40: Inmate George is on the phone. He tells you that he is having problems listening to his girlfriend. Then he tells you that the officer you just relieved for duty told him to tell you that if his phone conversation were to be interrupted you are to press the cutoff switch and turn it back on again.

There are only five phones in your unit, and they are all being used. You tell inmate George that if he was the only one using the phones, then, you would turn it off and on again.

He is very persistent in you turning off the phones. He tells you that there is a death in his family and he needs you to turn it off and back on again.

I need you to: In other words, I want you to.

You advise him that you cannot do that because everyone else's conversation will be cut off if you attempt to turn the phones off.

There comes a time when an inmate is upset during a phone conversation. He will let everyone around him know it also.

Talking loud, using offensive words in anger, and slamming the phone, is a sign that the situation might get ugly. So, you have to prepare to lock him down if the situation allows it.

If you must lock him down, approach him with caution. Would you let just anyone talk you into doing something they want you to do?

S41: Inmate Pill, who is assigned to your unit, is scheduled to be released today. A couple of nights ago, the inmates in the unit were making fun of inmate Pill. You told the inmates to stop laughing at him.

You tell them, how would you feel if people laughed at you all the time for no reason? Inmate Pill heard what you said but didn't acknowledge it.

He's an elderly man. Spends a lot of time alone and doesn't talk much. He listens when people talk and he certainly sleeps a lot. You can tell by looking at him that he always observes his surroundings.

Yesterday he showed you a paper with a drawing on it. It was a drawing of him entering the prison. In bold blue lettering, it said, "I am saved"

Today he shows you another sheet of paper with another drawing on it. It shows him leaving the prison system and entering the gates of heaven.

The drawing was very powerful. In bold letters, it read, "Thank you for saving me." He probably didn't have anyone who stood up for him before.

In the back of the drawing, he wrote his name and the name of a church. When you looked up the church's name on the internet, his name came up as the Pastor of the church.
He used to do volunteer work, and also donated his time to help underprivileged kids.

What was he in jail for? He was charged with murder.

His story was on TV the day he was released from prison. Everyone watched as he left and applauded him for his bravery. He was defending his wife, when a burglar broke into his home and tried to rape the woman that he spent more than thirty years of his life with.

While the man was raping inmate Pill's wife, Pill took a hammer and hit him over the head, causing a hole on the rapist's head. The rapist died instantly.

Inmate Pill is a free man now. He was in prison for a crime he didn't commit. It was later found that after further investigation, his wife was sickly, couldn't talk and had a heart attack the day the rape occurred.

Ever since then, inmate Pill has been lonely and depressed. The family of the man he allegedly killed had lots of money and fame. They paid the police department's Chief to make it look like inmate Pill committed a murder of a man who was only trespassing on his dwelling.

When it came to legal work, back then, inmate Pill didn't know how to defend himself.

No one gave him the opportunity to seek legal counsel. He stated that when he saw the man on top of his wife, he automatically hit him once, over the head with a hammer. The man was unarmed. Before leaving the prison, inmate Pill told you that you are the only officer who treated him like a human being.

Treat others how you want to be treated.

S42: It's after midnight. All the inmates in your unit appear to be sleeping. Before the inmates went to bed, you gave them a direct order to be quiet after the lights go off.

While conducting your next round, you observe an inmate sitting down on the floor in-between two bunks, talking to another inmate.

You tell the inmate that if he doesn't go back to his bunk you will have no choice but to have him go to disciplinary for disobeying a direct order. He tells you that he has a right to talk whenever he wants. And you can call whoever you want.

The inmate is being disrespectful.

You call your supervisor and she immediately responds. Upon the arrival of the supervisor, you tell her exactly what the inmate told you.

While your supervisor talks to the inmate, you are thinking that the inmate will leave in handcuffs and straight to disciplinary for disobeying your direct order.

The supervisor walks up to your desk and tells you that she spoke to the inmate. The inmate said he will not do that again. She gave him a pass, and tells you that if this happens again, just call her and the inmate will go to disciplinary.

If you are a corrupted officer, no one would trust you. If you're not careful, most of the inmates will probably take advantage of you.

If your supervisor lets certain inmates get away with doing stuff they are not supposed to do, you might not trust that supervisor. Or it could be that the supervisor might fear certain inmates.

Furthermore, you won't trust her to be your backup anymore. You might even let things go because you know which (her again) supervisor is on duty. We all need supervisors who are not afraid to stand-up for what's right.

An inmate broke a rule. Sometimes you can let it go, depending on the situation. But in this case, he disrespected the officer, and he got away with it.

Wouldn't you feel like the next time this happens, you will just let it go?

S43: Its Monday morning. Officer Davis just got out of work. However, he is still in uniform. He is in his favorite grocery store. He likes going there because the owner, Mr. Roberts, gives him free coffee.

A couple of people are in line, getting ready to pay for their groceries. Davis, can tell that they are in a hurry. He is also the last one online. The owner of the store sees that the only thing in his hand is a cup of coffee and some candy.

The owner immediately stops everyone online and calls Officer Davis over so he can pay for his items. Now, everyone on line appears to be upset.

While Officer Davis approaches the counter, a man standing in line tells him that he should be ashamed of himself for what he is doing. You skipped all of us just to pay for your stuff! The man said. We are in a hurry and some of us must go to work! The man shouted.

Officer Davis tells the man that it's not his fault the owner called him over.

I won't be long, Officer Davis said. The man tells Davis, that he is so upset that someone who works for our system treats people this way. While Davis pays for his items, and walks away, he tells the man to mind his own business.

The next day officer Davis is called into the supervisor's office. The supervisor tells Davis that he received a complaint from several people who saw him in a store with his uniform on. And he told one of them to mind their own business. "This doesn't look good," the supervisor said.

The man on line, who told him that he should be ashamed of himself, is an Administrative Lieutenant from this Prison.

Don't you have to be professional when your off duty? Do you think Officer Davis was ignoring the fact that other people were waiting online?

S44: An inmate approaches your desk and hands you a piece of paper. He says," I found this on the floor. "And then walks away. The letter reads: Dear Officer, yesterday while the other officer was in the unit, two inmates were fighting.

The officer didn't see the fight because he was in the restroom for at least ten minutes. No other officer was in the unit.

Before the officer left the rest room, everything was back to normal. "Like if nothing ever happened." When he made his rounds, he noticed that one of the inmates in the unit had a bloody nose. When the officer asked about the inmate's nose, the inmate told him he just had a nose bleed from playing an earlier game of basketball.

The officers smiled, and then he walked away.

Please look at the cameras and make sure this doesn't happen again. The inmate, who had the bloody nose, was involved in the fight.

When you look in your log book, you see nothing that says an inmate had a bloody nose, or that any inmate went to the medical office. And nothing that states the inmates was in the yard, at all. The inmates were in the unit the whole day.

Now that you have this piece of paper in your hands, what are you going to do? Will you try to track down the officer that took his time in the restroom when the incident happened? Will you verify the letter's statement?

What are you going to do with the inmate who gave you the letter? Will you put him down as the inmate you gave you the letter, and then walked away? Could you say, you just found it on the floor while making your rounds?

S45: Correction Officer Robert is off duty, and in civilian clothes. He decides to take a ride to his favorite grocery store that's located five minutes away from the prison.

While getting out of his car, he observes a robbery in progress, at the store. He is watching everything from the outside of the store's glass window. Since Robert is close to the window, the cashier looks at him like Robert just saved his life. However, the man with the gun is observed pointing the gun at the cashier's face.

The man with the gun, says, "Come inside, or I'll blow his head off." Robert quickly steps inside the store, with his hands up in the air and tells the gunman not to shoot.

Now that Robert is inside the store, the suspect can get a good look at him. He points the gun at Robert and says, walk to where the cashier is! Robert is very close to the exit door and he thinks he can make a break for it.

Robert quickly runs out the store and in to his vehicle. He just left the scene of a crime and he wants no part of it. Robert drives away like nothing ever happened. He doesn't mention any of this to anyone. Not even, the police or his supervisors.

Two days later, Robert is at work, making his rounds in a unit and watching TV with the inmates. A special bulletin appears from the news.

A grocery store clerk was shot in the face two days ago. The suspect is caught. The picture of the suspect is on TV. The news reporter says that the prison you work for is expecting his arrival.

A couple of minutes later, Robert received three new inmates in his unit. One of which is the suspect that killed the store clerk. While Robert gets the inmate's bed assignment ready, the suspect is looking at Robert like he knows him from somewhere.

The suspect quickly recognizes Robert and says, "That was you in the store." I almost shot you, officer. Too bad the store clerk is dead huh?

A couple of days later the suspect spoke with his lawyer, the Warden and the prison investigators. The suspect gave a description of the man that ran away from the scene at the store.

Through video surveillance footage, the investigators quickly found out that the person who fled the scene was one of their own.

Because the video was blurry, it only caught Robert's license plate, and the color of the vehicle. The suspect gave a statement to the investigators in return for a lesser sentence.

Officer Roberts was found guilty of being at the scene of the crime. He was fired from his job because he failed to report a crime he was a witness to.

Officer Robert is also being sued by the store clerk's family for not calling for help. He just left the store, ran and never even called anyone for assistance.

Why do you think Officer Robert didn't call for help? Could he have been scared? Maybe he had a dark past.

Since Robert didn't call for help, there's a possibility that the law enforcement community might think he was in on the robbery. How much effort does it take to call 911? If you were Officer Robert, how would you have changed this situation?

Do you have negotiation skills? What questions would you ask Officer Robert if you were the investigating officer?

S46: Officer Crystal is in a male inmate medical unit with ten inmates. Most of the inmates have psychiatric problems and cannot communicate well with others.

It is her responsibility to observe what's going on in the unit always. It's midnight. Most of the inmates are sleeping. Some are in bed reading a book or two. While Officer Crystal is at her desk, playing video games on her computer, an inmate walks up to her and tells her that there is another inmate in the restroom who he thinks is having a seizure.

She disregards what the inmate is telling her and tells him to walk away. Five minutes have gone by and she's still on the computer. She also forgets to make a couple of rounds. She's the kind of officer who just doesn't care about her job, and furthermore, about people's feelings.

What could happen if the inmate is having a seizure and Officer Crystal doesn't attend to him?

The inmates need medical attention.

Do you think someone like Officer Crystal should be working in a medical unit? Do you think her behavior can get an inmate or a staff member hurt?

S47: Officer Johnson is off duty and enjoying a nice weekend with his family. A couple of weeks ago he ordered a laptop computer from an online vendor.

He's been waiting for the laptop for quite a while now. In fact, it's two weeks late. He calls the vendor and demands that he gets at least a discount on his laptop for waiting so long. And he is also demanding a free two-year warranty on the laptop.

The representative informs him that the laptop is going to arrive late because of the holiday season and they can't give him any kind discounts. Johnson tells the representative that he is a Correctional Captain from the State Prison. If the representative does him a favor, and tries to speed up the process, Officer Johnson will make sure that he will get an interview for a possible future job in the prison.

Is Officer Johnson using his correctional status to get what he wants? Is Johnson's tittle Officer or Captain?

S48: Inmate Anderson approaches your desk and hands you a note. It reads: Dear officer, yesterday, I observed an inmate from this unit and one of your supervisors kissing in the blind spot area of the rest rooms.

She took him there because she knew the cameras weren't pointed in that direction. I think this happened around 3pm, while the other inmates were working in the kitchen area.

Your supervisor saw me and told me that if I told anyone about the incident she will deny it. And that she will make my life miserable if she found out I said anything.

I am scared that if I say anything to anyone I would get hurt by some of the inmates in this unit. I would like to remain anonymous.

The accusation is very serious. If a staff member is accused of kissing an inmate, most likely, the inmate that wrote the letter will have to come forward with his accusations. After all, he is a witness.

So, what's your next step? Are you going to confront your supervisor (the accused) about this first? Should you take this matter to the Prison's Investigations Unit? Your name is going to be on the statement as the person who received the letter.

What if you threw the letter away and you make believe the letter never existed?

The inmate that gave you the letter could tell another officer that he gave it to you and you did nothing about it.

S49: Its seven o'clock in the morning. You and your partner just pulled a twelve-hour shift and are getting ready to go home. Before you guys go home, you should wake up the inmates in order to get them ready for breakfast.

Your partner turns the lights on, and then makes an announcement for everyone to get up and get ready. Some inmates are still sleeping and don't want to get up. You and your partner are standing in the middle of the unit. While facing the inmates, your partner makes a second announcement. This time he yells, "Everyone get up for breakfast!"

All inmates are up but one. The inmate that is still in his bunk, tells your partner to shut up. Your partner quickly approaches the inmate's bunk, pulls the sheet off the inmate's body, and then quickly walks away.

The inmate immediately gets up from his bunk, angry and cursing at your partner for pulling the sheet off his body. All the inmates are laughing at him because he has no pants on just his underwear.

Was that an appropriate action from your partner? How would you handle this situation?

Picture yourself sleeping in bed. Suddenly, someone quickly pulls the sheets off from your body. Wouldn't you get upset or angry? The inmate is going to take that as disrespect. And other inmates would take that as you being a target.

S50: Officer Joker is off duty and enjoying a nice summer day in front of his house with his neighbor, Mr. Jones. Officer Joker and Mr. Jones like to share stories about the workplace. Mr. Jones tells Officer Joker that he knows a lot of people who work with him. But he didn't mention any names.

Officer Joker starts talking about a certain supervisor, Sergeant Packman, who he doesn't get along with. He tells Mr. Jones that this is the first time he is telling this story, because he might get in trouble for what he has done. Officer Joker admits to Mr. Jones that at certain times in the workday, Joker calls out the supervisor's name on the radio; even though nothing is going on to aggravate him. Officer Joker thinks it's funny.

Till this day, Sergeant Packman doesn't know who keeps calling him on the radio. Last week, two inmates were fighting in one of the units.

All supervisors, except Packman responded to the location. When the fight was over, Officer Joker called Sergeant Packman over the radio to respond immediately to the location to where the inmates were fighting.

Sergeant Packman was seen on video surveillance cameras running to the location. Officer Joker laughed at the thought of Sergeant Packman running. However, what happened next was not a joking matter.

While running, Sergeant Packman fell on the ground, hit his head, and sustained a broken left arm. Because of Officer Joker, Sergeant Packman is hurt and will have to go to the hospital.

Do you think it was necessary to have Sergeant Packman run to a false call?

A couple of days later, the prison received a phone call from an anonymous caller. The caller stated that Sgt. Packman sustained some injuries while he was running to a fight in progress. The caller also stated that the officer, who keeps calling Sgt. Packman on the radio, is Officer Joker.

A full investigation is underway. Officer Joker could be facing some charges, and termination from employment.

The anonymous caller stated that Sgt. Packman is his father.

What was Officer Joker's mistake?

Wouldn't you be angry if you found out that what happened to your father and the person who did it to him was your next-door neighbor?

S51: You're working a twelve-hour shift. From 7pm – 7am. While your supervisor makes his rounds in your unit, he tells you that the bottles of cleaning fluids are to be put away in the janitor's closet before midnight. The only items that can be left out during midnight is a broom and a dustpan.

No inmate should use the bottles after midnight. If they want to use them, they should wait until after 7am, when your relief arrives.

Inmate Carlos approaches your desk at 6:30am. He tells you that yesterday, while everyone was cleaning their cell, he was asleep. He had taken sleep medication which made him drowsy. However, now that he's wide awake, he would like to use the cleaning fluids to clean his cell. Since you feel sorry for him, you give him only one bottle. The one labeled, Ammonia.

Minutes later, inmate Carlos was seen by other inmates, emptying the bottle of ammonia into another inmate's water bottle.

Now that you have proof of the inmate's behavior, what are you going to do? What did your supervisor tell you not to do with the bottles? How would you discipline inmate Carlos since it was you, who broke the rules?

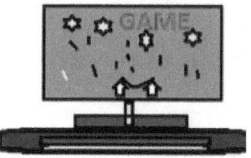

S52: Before your shift began, your supervisor made an announcement to the unit team officers. He said, "No officer can go on the internet for any inmate and give out any kind of information." No exception!

After your shift is over, you're officially on vacation.

Inmate Soto approaches your desk and asks you if you can go on the computer to verify a name and an address for him. You recognize the name and address, as the residence to an Assistant District Attorney. But you don't let him know that.

You then tell inmate Soto, that as per policy, you cannot look up any information on the internet. Inmate Soto replies with, "The other officer did it for me yesterday. Why can't you do it?" You tell inmate Soto that it's best for him to use the phone book that's in the unit or ask another inmate to get him the information he is looking for.

Inmate Soto is very persistent. He is aware that you like to play video games on the computer.

He mentioned that there is a website that you can go to where you get money by playing video games. All you have to do is play video games and if you win, your first prize is a one-hundred-dollar bill.

You believe him and start going to the video game site that inmate Soto told you about. Minutes later, your computer screen shows a malicious virus alert. You ignore the virus alert and continue to the website. The first page to the website appears to be a picture of a video game.

Five minutes have gone by and now your computer is frozen, showing naked pictures of a woman sitting on a couch. Now all the inmates are laughing because they know Inmate Soto played a trick on you.

You see, you told inmate Soto that you couldn't go online. However, when he told you it was a video game website, you were quickly interested. When you rebooted the computer, the virus was still there.

Suddenly you get a call from your Computer Security Department saying that they are receiving messages from their server, saying that your computer was downloading unauthorized material. The material is suspicious and it appears to be pornography.

You are now suspended without pay and under investigation until further notice, for downloading porn on the Institution's computer. How are you going to explain that one?

S53: Officer Alex is making his rounds. He is supposed to make his rounds twice an hour. It's after midnight and all the inmates appear to be sleeping on their bunks. While Officer Alex makes his second round, he hears an inmate saying, "I'm going to hang myself CO." Officer Alex disregards it and continues to make his rounds.

A couple of minutes later, Officer Alex sits by his desk. He hears an announcement on the radio telling him that his lunch relief is on the way. When the officer arrives to relieve him, he asks Officer Alex if he has anything to report before he takes over the unit. Officer Alex says, "Everything is fine." He quickly walks away from the unit and enters the staff break room.

While Officer Alex eats his meal, he turns his radio off. Two staff members are also in the break room. Suddenly, a medical emergency is called over the radio. The two staff members immediately left the break room and ran towards the direction of the emergency.

Officer Alex is now in route (walking slowly) to his unit. While doing so, he turns his radio back on, and sees that there are a lot of officers in front of his unit.

Why didn't you run to the medical emergency with us? One officer says. Officer Alex replied with, he didn't know what was going on since his radio was turned off. And that his lunch break is not going to be interrupted by an emergency call over the radio. We shouldn't be forced to stop what we are doing, just to run to an emergency.

I earned my lunch break just like any other staff members. Do you think the nurses get interrupted from their lunch break? I don't think so!

If you were the officer on the radio calling for help and you knew that officer Alex didn't come because he didn't care, what would you think of him? What if you were the one who needed medical attention?

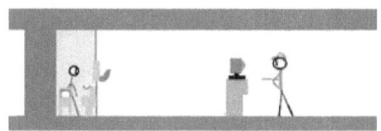

S54: Its 11pm on a Sunday. Officer Brown is working in the Medical Housing Unit. The inmates are sleeping and he is making his rounds. Suddenly, Officer Brown's supervisor tells him that a new inmate is going to be admitted in his housing unit.

A couple of minutes later, from across the hallway, Officer Brown observe two officers escorting the new inmate into cell number 10. He also noticed that the inmate was handcuffed behind his back.

Officer Brown thinks nothing of it because it's routine. He continued to make his rounds because the two officers didn't need any help with putting the new inmate in his cell. The two officers immediately left the housing unit without saying anything to Officer Brown. Not even the status of the inmate. Officer Brown continued to make his rounds. While making his rounds he observed that the inmate in cell 10 is lying on his bunk and with the sheets covering his body.

Everything looks good. The inmate looks like he is sleeping. Officer Brown continues to make his rounds.

It's almost quitting time. Seven o'clock, Monday morning. Officer Brown's log book says he completed all his rounds and that everything appeared secure throughout his tour.

Before Officer Brown packs his bags and gets ready to go home, the officer that relieves him, Officer Silva, should make a round to make sure everything is running smoothly. Officer Silva makes her rounds and discovers that the inmate in cell 10 is walking around in his cell with the handcuffs still, behind his back. She immediately alerts the supervisor on duty, and Officer Brown.

Officer Brown is shocked to find that the inmate was sleeping all night, but in handcuffs.

After watching the video surveillance footage, it was discovered that the two officers that brought the new inmate into the housing unit, escorted the inmate into his cell, but forgot to take off the handcuffs. The inmate is quickly transferred to another location in the building. Just in case the officers want to retaliate against him. Handcuffed, all night! He could have said something.

The Medical Housing Unit supervisor is requesting that Officer Brown and the two officers who brought the inmate in, be suspended immediately. At this point, it doesn't look good. An investigation has started about the new inmate being handcuffed.

Do you think Officer Brown should be blamed for someone else's actions?

He is not the one who left the handcuffs on the inmate. He made his rounds and didn't see anything out of the ordinary. Someone should take the blame, right? The supervisor is going down for it too. He was the one in charge. Officer Brown only got a suspension for not being observant enough.

S55: Officer Bambino is working the (SHU) Special Housing Unit. The inmates get along with him because he is friendly and gives the inmates extra food during lunch time.

Officer Bambino receives a call from his supervisor, stating that he will receive a new inmate in his unit, by the name of Cornwall.

This is inmate Cornwall's first time in prison. "He is here because he stole a State Trooper's vehicle." His supervisor says. "Treat him like any other inmate."

Nine months later.

The inmates and Officer Bambino are starting to treat Inmate Cornwall like one of the boys. Inmate Cornwall, likes the attention he is getting.

Officer Bambino has a habit of asking the inmates about their charges. He wants to confirm the conversation that took place with the inmate in question.

When inmate Cornwall was asked about his charges, he told Officer Bambino that he was busted for stealing a State Trooper's police car.

And is waiting to be moved to another prison where he is going to do the rest of his sentence.

Officer Bambino is satisfied with inmate Cornwall's statement, because he has heard about those cases before. He now considers inmate Cornwall one of the guys.

As time passes by, inmate Cornwall has been observing some unusual behavior coming from Officer Bambino. The inmates are saying that Officer Bambino is friendly with the inmates in the unit. He usually gives them whatever they want.

While walking in the pod, inmate Cornwall observes, one inmate smoking a cigarette in his cell. Another inmate was caught talking on a cell phone. Another was looking at porn magazines. Inmate Cornwall stood quiet about what he witnessed because he didn't want anyone to retaliate against him. He was offered a cigarette from one of the inmates but he declined.

While eating his breakfast, Inmate Cornwall heard a conversation between two inmates. "Officer Bambino is going to smuggle cartons of cigarettes, food from the outside, batteries and a couple of cell phones, in exchange for money and protection from other inmates."

Inmate Cornwall remembered all the information that was given to him by the other inmates. When he went back to his cell, he wrote a request to see the doctor. The request form was handed to Officer Bambino.

The next day, Inmate Cornwall was called to see the doctor. He was the only one who left the Special Housing Unit. When inmate Cornwall arrived at the Doctor's office, he requested to see the Warden.

The Warden spoke to inmate Cornwall about the suspicious activity that was taking place in Officer Bambino's unit. He also took inmate Cornwall's accusation very seriously, and then told inmate Cornwall that the matter will be investigated. But he needed proof to back up the accusation. Inmate Cornwall gave the Warden the notes that he had saved under his mattress. Everything that Officer Bambino has done is documented on a note pad. And it will be used as a legal document.

Inmate Cornwall never returned to the Special Housing Unit. As far as everyone knows, Cornwall transferred to another prison after he finished seeing the doctor.

During the investigation, Officer Bambino was caught smuggling a carton of cigarettes, two cell phones, batteries for a small hand-held radio, and a bag of marijuana with an inmate's name on it.

What happened to Inmate Cornwall?

He was an Undercover Agent (Special Taskforce) for the Department of Justice. He was investigating corruption within the Justice System. Agent Cornwall stated that working undercover as an inmate was one of the most dangerous assignments that was ever given to him.

The inmate that gave inmate Cornwall the information on Officer Bambino was immediately given his release papers because he was cooperating with investigators.

Officer Bambino is in prison serving a ten-year sentence for his conduct and malicious behavior, Introduction to narcotics in a prison, and for giving false statements to the investigators. All the inmates in Officer Bambino's care were interviewed.

Because of their statements, Officer Bambino was later brought up with more charges.

S56: For the past three months, a couple of inmates have filled complaint forms because they did not receive their mail envelopes from their family and friends.

Officer Jackson works in unit 7. The inmates in unit 7 have been complaining to Officer Jackson about their mail. Officer Jackson tells them that he has nothing to do with the mail since he is only the unit officer. He also tells them that anyone who has a problem with the mail must put in a request or complaint form to find out what's going on with their mail.

Unit officers are required to inspect incoming mail before they hand it over to the inmates. Some envelopes are marked: fragile, immediate attention, pictures only, priority or sensitive material.

On December 22nd, all the inmates in unit 7 were expecting to receive mail from their family and friends. Only a few received their envelopes. Suddenly, Officer Jackson received a phone call from his wife telling him that she felt sick, and that she was on her way to the hospital. Officer Jackson quickly left the prison to go help his wife.

While driving to the hospital, he failed to stop at a stop sign. He was then stopped by a police officer who observed Officer Jackson pass the sign and abruptly changing (swerve) directions from lane to lane.

While standing by the passenger door, the police officer noticed a couple of open beer bottles sitting on the front passenger side. Officer Jackson is getting nervous and quickly explains to the officer that he is on his way to the hospital, and that he is sorry for not stopping at the stop sign. The police officer tells Officer Jackson to turn off the engine, get out of the car and to stand behind the trunk of the vehicle.

The police officer also tells Officer Jackson that he is going to check the inside of his vehicle because when Officer Jackson was driving, it appeared that he was swerving and wanted to see if there was anything else he (the police officer) should be concerned about.

Officer Jackson told the police officer that he had only a little to drink. But he has permission to check the car. After the cop checked the car, Jackson was tested for alcohol. Jackson failed the test. His blood alcohol level was higher than the state minimum.

The police officer arrested Officer Jackson for DWI; more charges are pending because the police officer found at least two hundred envelopes in Officer Jackson's trunk.

All the envelopes had the return address to the prison where Johnson worked. None of the envelopes had Officer Jackson's name on it.

S57: The inmates in Officer Carter's unit know him as one of the many officers who sleep on the job. A couple of days ago Officer Carter's supervisor warned him that if he gets caught sleeping on the job again he's going to be facing disciplinary action and up to dismissal.

Today is inmate inspection day. Officer Carter is getting ready to inspect inmate Jackson's cell for contraband. Inmate Jackson is one of the inmates who occasionally, observe Officer Carter sleeping on the job. But never says anything because Officer Carter is a cool officer.

While conducting the inspection in inmate Jackson's cell, Officer Carter observes a white powdery substance in a small plastic bag, under inmate Jackson's mattress. He also observes a couple of rolled up paper in the form of cigarettes that appear to be marijuana.

Officer Carter informs inmate Jackson that he is going to the Disciplinary Unit (The Hole) for the contraband found in his cell until they test the contraband for drugs.

Inmate Jackson informs Officer Carter that if he tells on him, he will have no choice but to tell his supervisor that he was caught sleeping again, during their recreation time.

If Officer Carter sends the inmate to the Hole for further investigation, he could save himself from being fired, or suspended.

But, what if he lets the inmate go with a warning? What is Officer Carter going to do with the drugs he found in Inmate Jackson's cell?

What would you have done if you were Officer Carter?

S58 You just completed nine months on the job. Today is your first day of training in another area of the facility. Officer Mack is your FTO (Field Training Officer). While going on a lunch break with Officer Mack, you pull on a door that's near the staff dining room. You open it and it appears that the inside of that room is dark. You try to turn the lights on because you think it's a breach of security by leaving a door unlocked in an unsecure area.

Officer Mack tells you; don't worry about that door, it's always unlocked. You follow your instincts and attempt to turn the light switch on. It doesn't work, so you proceed to walk towards the dining room. On the way to the dining room, you hear voice coming from the same room you just left. It sounds like two people giggling and whispering.

You go back to investigate the noise, and then find a female inmate with her jail uniform on and a coworker, (Officer Luis) lying under a table with a couple of blankets on the floor.

The inmate is surprised to see you and Officer Luis, looks at you and tells you that you didn't see or hear anything. Officer Luis also states, in a loud voice, Mack! I told you not to let anyone else in here! Now, you got me in trouble.

Who knew that Officer Luis was in the dark room with an inmate?

Now what? Are you going to report the incident? So, what's your next step? You better think quickly!

S59: As per facility rules, when a nurse is in your unit, you are not allowed to distribute, hold medication for any inmate or give advice to an inmate about what he/she should take for their medical condition.

You are assigned to a medical unit. While the nurse is in your unit distributing the medication to the inmates, she calls out inmate Holder's name, but he doesn't answer.

You know inmate Holder is sleeping because when you last made your rounds, you observed him looking at you from his bunk, then he told you that he doesn't want you to wake him up when the nurse gets there.

You informed inmate Holder that if he refuses medical attention he should tell the nurse himself. The nurse tells you that inmate Holder needs to take his medication, and then hands it to you in a little plastic cup, so you can give it to inmate Holder when he wakes up. The nurse quickly exits your unit and says, thank you.

You are in possession of inmate Holder's medication. And it's in front of your desk, where every inmate can see it. Inmate Jones, a trustee, approaches your desk and notices that you're very busy. He asks if he can take inmate Holder's medication to him since he is his bunk buddy. You give inmate Jones the medication and tell him that he needs to make sure it gets to him. Inmate Jones walks away with the little cup in his hands and smiles at you saying, thank you.

The unit telephone rings, you pick it up and it's one of your buddies from work. The conversation lasted about 5 minutes.

Another inmate tells you that he saw inmate Jones drink the medication you gave him, which belong to another inmate. You quickly wake up inmate Holder to find out if he took the medication that inmate Jones was supposed to give him. He replied with, I never got my medication. I was sleeping.

So, you gave an inmate medication that didn't belong to him. How are you going to explain this one? Were you supposed to take the medication from the nurse?

If inmate Holder told you not to wake him up for medication, why hold his medicine? Inmate Holder can write a grievance against you. And if Inmate Jones gets sick because of the medication you gave him to hold, he can end up in the hospital. You can lose your job for not following policy.

S60: It's almost bedtime. The inmates are tired after coming from the recreation yard. They also want to go to bed and relax.

Your Captain enters your unit and gives all the inmates a direct order to sit down in the Day room because he should deliver an important message. As well as receive feedback.

The captain stated:

Everyone here is aware that a cell phone was found in cell#8, yesterday. We are investigating and I need everyone's cooperation. The faster we take care of this; the faster you guys can go to bed.

All the inmates were interviewed individually by the Captain as you observed.

One inmate told the Captain that Officer Delco (your best friend from your job), was the one who brought in the cell phone.

The Captain informed the inmates that the matter will be investigated and they are not to talk about the investigation to any outside person. Once this matter is resolved, this unit will get an extra hour of TV, an extra hour of recreation, and extra cartons of milk on their breakfast tray.

You cannot tell Officer Delco about what you have heard. The investigation is still pending. And now, you should make believe you don't know anything about it.

Will you tell your buddy about the investigation and what he has been accused of?

In closing, I hope you find this information helpful and valuable in preparation for your first day on the job as a corrections officer determining if a career in corrections is a good fit for you.

This book is also for current officers looking for more information to continue to guide them in their correctional career. And for anyone who just wanted to know what it's like to work at a jail settling.

To those who put their lives on the line, thank you for the work that you do.

www.ingramcontent.com/pod-product-compliance
Lightning Source LLC
Chambersburg PA
CBHW030750180526
45163CB00003B/971